Standing at the Crossroads

Phil O'Keeffe

STANDING
AT THE
CROSSROADS

PHIL
O'KEEFFE

First published in 1997 by
Brandon Book Publishers Ltd
Dingle, Co. Kerry, Ireland

British Library Cataloguing in Publication Data is available for this book.

ISBN 0 86322 231 5

Brandon Book Publishers receive financial assistance from
An Chomhairle Ealaíon/The Arts Council, Ireland

Cover photography: O'Connell Street, Dublin 1942,
Fr Browne S.J. Collection; Three Friends, Dublin 1952, Patricia Griffin
Cover design by The Public Communications Centre Ltd, Dublin
Typeset by Seton Music Graphics, Bantry, Co. Cork
Printed by Colourbooks Ltd, Dublin

Burrowing in the recesses of my mind
Plundering my store of memories,
Standing at crossroads long gone,
I have paid my dues.

Acknowledgements

To Peter Malone, my editor at Brandon, who was always at the end of the telephone to listen and encourage, and Terry Mhic Gearailt for her work on the manuscript. Steve, Bernard, Linda and Bríd at Brandon helped set the book in motion. To my five children who supported me all the way. And to my sisters and extended family, thank you.

APRIL 1997

Contents

1. The Road is Wide — 1

2. Weaving the Threads — 13

3. Poor People, Good People — 27

4. Be Prepared — 38

5. The Long Days of Lent — 47

6. Wicklow — 57

7. Invitation to Tea — 63

8. Moving On — 76

9. Taking Flight — 86

10. New Horizons — 94

11. Are There Roads in Rome? — 105

12. Standing at the Crossroads — 124

13. Decisions — 144

14. The Chosen Way — 160

15. New Beginnings — 173

1

The Road is Wide

IT WAS 1945, and the war was nearly over. I had finished my
secretarial course at the VEC's College of Commerce on the
Rathmines Road. They had been two years of learning and fun.
The first year we wore navy gym-slips, with a wine-coloured sash
when we sang in *feiseanna*, and graduated to navy office-coats in our
second year to give us the feel of a real office. We had left the regi-
mentation of our schooldays behind us and were treated as young
adults, addressed as 'Miss' at all times, and prepared in a practical
way for the ordinary life of an office. All note-taking, essays,
assignments and tests were done on foolscap paper the size of office
stationery, and our work had to be filed properly in folders which I
carried importantly, grasped tightly to my breast.

Our staff teacher had qualifications in both Pitman and Gregg
shorthands and taught us the skills we would need in our working lives.

'Girls,' she said, 'I've taken the best from both systems. Pitman is
the most reliable for transcription, so we will concentrate on that,
but Gregg gives fluency to the wrist, which you need when taking
rapid dictation.' So we took our shorthand tuition, pencils – HB
pencils – poised, using Mr Pitman's straight strokes for accuracy and
Mr Gregg's flowing curves for fluidity.

Our introduction to the world of touch-typing was on faceless
typewriters, their key-boards covered by a wooden frame to begin with.

'Place your hands on the home keys, and with the first finger of
the left hand resting on "f", strike it,' and we all struck in unison.
'Move it to "r"' – and at this our fumbling and our sneaky looking
under the wooden frame brought the ire of Miss Gunning crashing

down on our heads – 'and strike it,' she cried, but the striking was never quite in harmony.

'With the first finger of the right hand resting on "j" strike it, and move it to "u" and strike it,' and on and on we went until she was sure we could be trusted not to look at the keys and the frames were removed. She assured us we would never need look at the keys again, but she vigilantly watched for straying eyes as we copied exercise after exercise from the propped-up typewriting manuals, and learned how to correspond with the lowest citizen and the most lordly bishop. Bookkeeping I cheerfully hated and I ploughed my way reluctantly through entries into journals, petty-cash books, ledgers, debits and credits and the horrendous balancing statements, which gave me nightmares.

Our school hours were official office hours and, besides our commercial subjects, our time was filled with lectures on English, Irish, and commercial art, when we made glorious posters for everything under the sun under the tuition of a feathery, white-haired lady who found talent in every one of her students and encouraged us to experiment with colour. Neither was our physical education neglected, and we climbed the parallel bars and made sprawling attempts to jump over the vaulting horse while our instructor, Kathleen O'Rourke, encouraged, berated and despaired of the lot of us. Religion was not forgotten in the Vocational Education Committee's new approach to post-primary teaching, and we had a weekly religion class supplied by the Carmelites from their house of studies in Rathgar.

A few weeks after graduating I brought a slip of paper from the College of Commerce home to my mother. It was May, and every effort was being made by the college to ensure that each student was 'placed'.

I liked the sound of an office set in the countryside and so I had opted for a job at Killeen Paper Mills. Miss Healy, my staff teacher, had already tried to dissuade me.

'Do you really want to work so far outside the city?' she asked, looking at me long and hard. 'It's in a big country house away from the streets and the roads.'

'I like the country!' I protested stoutly. The challenge of the unknown and the feeling of doing something different appealed to me, but the self-same unknown was worrying my mother as she watched me prepare for the interview.

'Where,' she said when she had read the slip, 'where in God's name is the Killeen Paper Mills?'

'Somewhere near the Halfway House,' I hedged. At least the Halfway House was something she could get her bearings on. 'It's out the Long Mile Road.' My mother sat down on the chair beside the kitchen table and looked at me. I could see she was troubled.

'That's open country,' she said, an anxious frown creasing her forehead. 'How do they expect you to get there?'

'I'm sure it's not that far. I can walk.' My mother raised her eyebrows at my certainty, but she didn't pursue the argument further.

'You'll wear the pale pink blouse with the costume?' she said. The costume was my first grown-up outfit. In preparation for all the interviews I was going to get, or at least she hoped I would get, she had gone to the Woollen Mills on Ormond Quay and bought a costume-length of wine-coloured cloth. I wasn't sure how many clothes coupons she had to give for it, but it would be considerably less than the twenty-five required for a lady's coat or the thirty-two coupons demanded for a man's, a price which caused my mother to thank her lucky stars that she had no young men to dress. My mother consulted the assistant as to the colour, quality and wearability of the material and was assured that it was good value for money. I never dreamed of questioning her choice, but it did strike me when the whole outfit was complete that everything suited my colouring.

I did, however, have a say in the style. When I was fourteen, before I took up my scholarship with the VEC, I had spent six months working with a tailor, so I deemed I had a superior knowledge of the tailoring trade. I impressed the dressmaker, my mother and myself with my grasp of linings, inter-linings, collar facings and buttonhole twists, and I knew exactly where I wanted the jacket hem to end and how many pleats I wanted in the skirt.

'It doesn't matter how many you want,' the dressmaker had said waspishly, 'you can only have as many as the amount of material you have bought. There is a war on.'

I wasn't all that nervous on the day I took the interview: it was nearly like a game, a challenge to prove that I could get the job if I put my mind to it. And I did put my mind to it. Everything that I had been told to do when we had rehearsed interviews in the College of Commerce, I did. To satisfy my mother I had carried my Cuban-heeled shoes in a paper bag, so they would not be dusty when I put my foot across the threshold of the managing director's office. I straightened the seams of my tan lisle-thread stockings just before I turned in from the country lane, smoothed my hair and perched my pink beret on my head, and I felt confident as I swung my handbag, which held my lace hankie, the card for the interview and the money for the bus-fare home.

Things went well at the interview. I asked all the questions we had been told to ask about lunch hours and the sacred holiday pay and more importantly how many days holiday I was entitled to and when I could take them, which seemed a bit premature to me but it was just as well to get it all straight. I remembered to appear confident and not cheeky, so I asked where the toilet facilities were, mindful of the fact that this was an office set in the country and facilities might be limited. Everybody would have been proud of me as I sat bolt upright in my chair and didn't cross my legs. I managed to look intelligent and nod my head in the right places; I concentrated when a letter was dictated to me and wrote little squiggles of longhand in the margins to remind me of unfamiliar words like wood-pulp and various names of packages which were known to the managing director and which he forgot were new to me. I click-clacked at reasonable speed on an ancient typewriter at a desk in the outer office and hoped they would allocate me a more up-to-date one if I got the job.

I did not say 'sir' once. Aunt Kathleen, who was my father's sister and an authority on etiquette, thought that all older males in authority expected it and warned me away from the practice. 'Hold your head up,' she once instructed me, 'look people straight in the eye and adddress them as Mr So-and-So – never as "sir",' and she had stuck her nose in the air; a good noble Roman nose on her side of the family, she was fond of stating. I suspected she used glue to anchor her glasses behind her ears. She never touched them or her hair while in company and disdained permanent waves and those who had recourse to them. Her hair was covered with a fine silk net, and not a strand out of place beneath the prim brown hat.

'Twenty-two and six per week is what we pay,' the managing director announced in his brusque English accent, ruffling through papers without looking at me. 'Is that satisfactory to you?' and he glanced up quickly when I didn't reply. Of course it was satisfactory, but I had expected him to say, 'We will consider your application and let you know.' The fact that he was offering me the job on the spot was slow to sink in. I wasn't sure how to react. Should I say I would consider his offer and let him know?

'We work a five and a half-day week, and we start at 9.30 a.m. sharp.' Maybe he sensed my uncertainty because he rose from the chair and, clutching a sheaf of papers to him, said, 'We'll see you in two weeks' time then.' He made no move to extend his hand, and I felt I was being summarily dismissed. I rose to my feet and gathered my paper bag and my handbag and pulled on my gloves. Always be polite, was ringing in my ears. I extended my gloved hand – a lady's privilege – and heard myself saying 'thank you' in what I thought was a gracious manner. He followed me to the door and informed the staff in the outer office that I would be joining them in a fortnight.

'You're jaded.' My mother took one look at me and put the kettle on the gas, plumping up the cushion on the old sofa and sitting me down. My feet were sore because in my excitement at being told I had the job I had forgotten to take the Cuban-heeled shoes off until I was half-way down the Long Mile Road, and a big water-blister was forming on my right heel.

'I got the job.' My soreness and tiredness evaporated at the memory of the salary I had been offered.

So now, a month after graduation my mother shook me gently as I lay curled up in bed, but I burrowed my head further into the bedclothes.

'It's seven o'clock,' she whispered, 'the bus goes at quarter to eight. You don't want to be late on your first morning. Shsh,' she said then as I bolted upright, 'the others don't have to get up yet. Keep quiet.' I crept from the bedroom which I shared with two of my sisters, clutching the clothes I had laid out in readiness the night before.

'You have to eat something,' my mother said as I toyed with the porridge she had spooned out for me. 'Maybe you'd prefer a piece of fried bread. At least that's not rationed anymore.' She heated beef dripping until it spat and sizzled in the iron frying-pan and filled the kitchen with its lovely warm smell. She grumbled as she twisted the gas-knob, trying to coax another glimmer from the gas which was not due to come on until eight o'clock, then she crowed gently as the flame suddenly flared. 'Somebody got the Gas Company alarm wrong again. Maybe the war's over!'

But I didn't want to eat the fried bread any more than the porridge. I had cobbly-wobbles in my tummy and I was already all-thumbs as I stood up buttoning my blouse and unravelling the furry pipe-cleaners which I had put in the ends of my hair the night before to give it a curl for my very first day in my new job.

The skipping I had done in the lane when I had left the gates of the mill behind me on the day of the interview was far from my thoughts as I entered the office on that first morning. I had a thumping headache and a feeling of apprehension. For all my enthusiasm for the countryside, I was tired from the long walk and wanted to sit down somewhere for a rest. The secretary of the company who had nodded to me on the day of the interview when the managing director had thrown introductions around, saw me coming and held the door open for me. He smiled and bade me good morning reassuringly. I was early and in the absence of the rest of the office staff he showed me where to hang my coat. I unfolded the new navy office-coat – the regulation uniform of all clerical staff in every firm – and I sat at the desk he showed me. Same old rackety typewriter. I reminded myself that the firms who supplied typewriters were English, and new typewriters would have been very far down on the list of commodities which came through our ports.

The secretary disappeared into his office which he shared with the accountant. His courtesy and refinement of manner were a direct contrast to the managing director's, whose cranky voice came clearly from his office as he told a demanding customer in no uncertain tones that there was a war on and he couldn't just have anything he wanted. His irate tongue was something I would soon get used to.

'His bark is worse than his bite,' the accountant said as he passed by my desk, nodding towards the manager's office. But to me he was different; he was a foreigner and we didn't come across many foreigners. He ran his mills with a brisk efficiency and, right from my very first morning, he rushed through his dictation of letters and shouted strange addresses of places in England to me.

I was being trained to take the place of the other shorthand-typist, Máire, who had given notice that she was leaving to enter a convent. She dealt with the managing director's manner with a calmness which I watched and admired. She never let him ruffle her, and because of that he thought the world of her. Máire had already decided what she wanted to do with her life, and this clear-sightedness was the basis of her efficiency. I had no clear-cut vision of my future as yet. I was happy with my position on the first rung of the ladder, and for the moment this saw me typing invoices, transcribing short-hand sometimes furiously dictated, and battling with the old warhorse of a typewriter, my constant and most cantankerous workmate.

I swung into the routine of working life, rising at seven in the morning before anyone else was up and leaving the house half an hour later. Our house lay between Cork Street, which led to the city, and the Back of the Pipes, an alleyway which led directly to Dolphin's Barn, a lovely, bustling village set on a crossroads. I walked quickly up the Back of the Pipes, meeting a stream of people coming against me with heads bent. Intent on the factory-horns which sounded at five- or ten-minute intervals, men and women, old and young, were rushing to clock in at the city factories before the last, lonely siren faded into silence. I was going against the tide.

I stepped on to the cobbled streets of the village, skirted the gentlemen's toilet which stood on a concrete island and walked up to the iron railings which bordered the ancient Celtic cross belonging to Dolphin's Barn Church. The bus from the city centre which took me to my new job stopped here.

I leaned up against the railings and waited. Facing me was the elegant building of the Royal Bank of Ireland, on the corner of the Hollow. I had never been inside a bank, though as inquisitive youngsters we had often stopped to peer through the glass-panelled doors at the polished wooden floors, the brass railings at the counters and the padded seats for important customers. I loved to see the porter in his braided uniform doff his cap when a customer entered or sweep the door open with a courtly gesture when somebody came out, though he was very quick to chase us away. I gazed across at the bank on those early mornings as the lights came on in the bow-fronted windows, and I wondered if I would one day marry a bank manager and would I ever have enough money for a bank account?

I missed the trams which used to run across Dolphin's Barn. In the early days of the trams, Dolphin's Barn had been the terminus, the busy crossroads between town and country, until the increase in traffic forced the Dublin United Tramway Company to stretch the line further on to Rialto. Travelling by tram was always dignified, much more so than on a crowded steamy bus, but the sound of their clanging had died some four years earlier when the last tram from Rialto disappeared.

My father had loved the trams. He had died just a few months earlier, and we had been robbed of a generous, loving parent whom I would love to have had beside me now as I started to make my way in an adult world. He would have been proud of the progress I had made, but would have countered with stories of the old days and made astute observations between the then and the now.

'The horse-trams,' he used to say, 'were the best of the lot. A pair of horses stepping it out to bring a tramload of people out beyond there to the country on an outing – ah, nothing better. They were slow,' he would concede, 'but then life was slow, and not all hustle and bustle like it is today.' And as I waited for my bus I remembered the grip he used keep on our hands as we waited opposite Dolphin's Barn Church while the electrified tram on its shiny tracks breasted the rise just past the bank opposite.

The tram somehow added to the graciousness of the old village. The new city buses snorted fumes as they slithered into the channels at the footpaths, scattering mud and dust, while the tram stood proudly on the crown of the road, commanding its space, its arrival and departure heralded with clanging bells and rattling wheels. It demanded to be heard as its overhead wires arced and buzzed and the bogeys clattered over the tracks. On fine sunny mornings we used dash to the open seats on the top deck, the wind whipping through our hair as we were jostled and bumped when the tram gathered speed, and the empty wooden seats clapping in unison.

But it was not a horse and carriage from the old Halfway House, nor yet a humming, singing tram which was my mode of transport to my new job. It was 'the country bus', the low green single-decker bus which rattled up the Crumlin Road, its one or two passengers settling into a doze for the extra forty winks they had been denied by their early morning journey.

After the first day, when I had felt terribly alone after the bus deposited me at the Halfway House, I began to enjoy the long walk to work in the fine summer mornings. The Long Mile Road was uncharted country. The country bus continued past the Cuckoo's Nest and on to Tallaght, where we picked blackberries and fraughans in summer, but no bus went out the Long Mile which led to the busy Naas Road and on to the flat plains of Kildare. Every morning my mother sprinkled me with Holy Water to keep me safe while I negotiated the junction at the top of the road, with another half mile of country lane before the gates of the mill would offer me sanctuary.

The Halfway House, the starting point of my journey, was a bona fide public-house much used by men who wished to drink outside normal drinking-hours. My father had explained it to us on one of our Sunday walks when we were children. Years before, he told us, travelling had been on horseback or by horse-drawn carriage, and inns were set up to facilitate the traveller, who had the right to demand food and drink at any time. The custom had been modified over the years, of course, and the bona fides of someone seeking drink had now to be determined by how far he had travelled. As I set out for the office, I would conjure up foaming horses, caped travellers, and ladies in flowing dresses and dark cloaks, lifting dainty, satin-shod feet over muddy, rutted roadways.

Trailing blackberry bushes grew along the uneven clay path at the side of the road, and the scent of dead-man's blossom hung like musk in the still air of early morning. Tendrils of golden laburnum twined among the lilac bushes on the hedges of the little cottages dotted along the road. The ditches on both sides rioted in white, yellow, orange and pink. Cowslips grew in bunches in the open fields. I revelled in the feeling of being in the country, though my heart stopped every time I passed a cottage, fearful of the shrill barking of dogs. I put a brave face on it as I marched past, looking back over my shoulder to make sure my heels weren't their target. A cat padded ahead of me, stealthily moving with up-raised tail, a heart-shaken, back-broken mouse firmly clasped in his jaws. The cat stopped to stare at me, daring me to rescue his forlorn prey.

Motorcars swished past, their drivers, like horses, scenting the open road ahead. None stopped or slowed. I was wary anyway, and well warned about slowing motorcars and suave individuals with gracious manners, and my mind filled with thoughts of being whisked away to an unknown country as part of the white slave trade.

'Whoah there, take it aisy.' A horse and cart slowed beside me. It was the milkman.

'Want a lift a bit of the way?' He stared straight ahead over the horse's head. 'You've a long ways to go yet.'

'Thank you very much,' I said as I placed my foot on the iron step at the side of the dray and swung up beside him.

'Steady now,' he shouted and his words could have been directed at me rather than the horse as I wobbled into position beside him. The milk-cans jangled behind us as we trotted away from the path.

'You're makin' your way up beyond the road,' he said. 'I seen ye for the past week.' I told him where I was working.

'Fine,' he said, 'fine in the summer anyway.' That was the extent of our conversation: enough by way of explanation and the reason for his stopping. As the weeks followed, he slowed each morning if he saw me on the road, but never waited for me. If my bus was late, it was too bad.

When the milkman let me down, I continued my walk to work, soaking in the sounds of summer: the crickets chirping loudly behind the hedges, the uneasy croaking of frogs in the muddy waters of the ditch, and the cock's trumpeting 'cock-a-doodle-do'. Except for the occasional 'whoosh' of a motorcar as it swept past, there were no alien noises to drown the voices of nature, though I had to remain perfectly still to hear the corncrake creaking in the long grasses and the cuckoo with its echoing, changing call required total concentration. When a heat-haze rose from the fields to muffle far-away sounds, it was difficult to be really sure that it was his elusive voice I heard.

As I stood on the roadside with my ear cocked, I heard another sweet sound approaching. It was Máire, my senior in the office, and she was singing. Like me Máire was a past student of Rathmines College of Commerce, and two years previously in the Student

Union elections we had been exhorted to 'Vote for the girl with the golden voice – let her use it on your behalf'. I envied her that glorious, soaring sound which now preceded the creaking of the bicycle which I saw coming towards me.

'*A éinín, a éinín, in áirde ar an gcrann, Is binn liom, is binn liom, is binn liom do rann,*' she carolled. 'Little birds in the bushes, I love your sweet song,' she sang, but I could have sworn the birds grew silent in order to listen to her.

'Want a carry on the bike?' she said as she slowed beside me.

'I don't think so,' I said dubiously. I'd been carried on the crossbars of bicycles in the country but never on the back-carrier.

'Sit side-saddle,' she commanded as she brought the bike to the ditch at the side of the road. She stood astride the bike as I sat on the carrier and gripped the saddle tightly, balancing my handbag full of lunch somewhere between my knees. With her right foot on the pedal and her left on the ditch, she pushed off. She strained at the pedals as we wound back and forth across the road. She was just beginning to find her rhythm when the sound of a car-engine panicked her into seeking the comparative safety of her own side of the road. I put one foot to the ground to avoid the ditch but the cog-wheel caught me, thus destroying my good pair of stockings. As I unbalanced, Máire's feet slid from the pedals and we fell in an undignified heap on the side of the road.

Máire had to be in the office and couldn't waste any more time with me; she hauled the bike to an upright position, dusted herself off and pedalled furiously away. I watched her as she disappeared, hand outstretched in signal as she reached the junction. Her election poster had been designed by Ronnie Masterson, who later became a famous actress on the Abbey stage, and Máire could surely have found a career on stage, too, but a very different destiny was now beckoning her. I wondered what convent thought it could hold that voice so full of promise, or curb that bubbling, independent spirit.

The summer sped by. I soon found my feet in my new job and enjoyed working in a big country house, where the cows poked their heads in through the lower windows and snorted typing paper onto the floor. On fine days I loved to take my lunch sandwiches and sit on the grassy hump beside the bridge which spanned the junction of the river Camac and the canal. Sometimes I would pore over the newspapers which were full of the Allied armies' victories and the devastation wreaked by six years of war. Hitler was dead and the war in Europe was over, and on the other side of the world the Americans had dropped the atom bomb on Japan. I was seventeen and all of these things seemed very far away.

2
Weaving the Threads

MY MOTHER HAD never forgotten the bout of double pneumonia I had suffered when I was seven years old, and she had no intention of letting me forget it either.

'If you got up ten minutes earlier in the morning, you wouldn't be hopping about on one leg like a hen on a hot griddle. Stay where you are; I'll have this ready for you in a minute.'

'I'll miss the bus,' I wailed as she started whipping the raw egg which now replaced the Parrish's Food and cod liver oil which had been poured down our throats as children. Ignoring my agitation, she added a tablespoon of milk to the mixture and began to heat it in the little saucepan, watching carefully lest it boil because that would cook the egg and the whole thing would lose its goodness, according to her. This gave me time to grab my coat from the coat hanger in the hall, where she followed me, still stirring. 'I've added a drop of sherry,' she said. 'Drink it all.' She handed the cup back to me to drain the dregs. The sherry was added insulation against the early morning cold and wet. 'An egg-flip is not going to protect you if you get a bad dose of 'flu,' my mother said anxiously, and I knew she was right.

My mother worried more about my early mornings than about the war's ending or the rationing we were still going through. When autumn rain began to lash the open road, I dragged on Wellington boots and carried a change of shoes and clothing with me, but now the cold air spat frost and the wind turned my umbrella inside out, and I began to feel a little like Padraic Colum, 'tired of the crying wind and the lonesome hush'. I wondered what I should do for the future.

My father's death had drawn us all closer together, and throughout his illness my two older sisters, near in age, had already been shouldering some of the responsibility of providing for four younger sisters. Madge, tall and slim with an abundance of waist-length auburn hair, was my mother's right hand. She took on the duties of knitting cardigans and jumpers, checking ration-books, allocating household chores and keeping us all in line, with the efficiency, good humour and confidence of a born manager. By the time I had left school, she had the first Raleigh bicycle in the house, and needed it to get to the draper's shop on the Quays where she was apprenticed. We all took turns on the bike during our Sunday walk, and I was pushed, wobbled, and finally propelled into solo flight along the Tallaght Road, with Madge and Babs one on each side of me, their long legs trying to keep up with my speeding wheels. When they left my side I panicked, pulled the front brake and catapulted with instinctive accuracy into the roadside ditch.

Babs, flaxen-haired like the maternal grandmother we never knew, was our bookworm and turned her cleverness and constant reading to good account when she succeeded by dint of studying and hard work in securing a clerical job in the Civil Service. Competition for these jobs was then at its fiercest, because many of the temporary staff who had been recruited during the Emergency years to cope with the various rationing procedures were eager to be made permanent, now that examinations were again being held.

The lean years of my father's unemployment before the war and then his long illness and death in the year war ended, had been the greatest challenge of my mother's life. Her own mother had died when she was fourteen years old, and though she herself was only a child she had been expected to leave aside all thoughts of outside employment and devote herself to housekeeping for her father, a drayman with Arthur Guinness, Son & Company. She had no experience of the world of work. She was a country girl first and foremost, proud of our Wicklow ancestry on both sides of her family and on my father's side too. We lived surrounded by a long-tailed family of cousins who lived in and around Thomas Court, Thomas Court Bawn and South Earl Street in the Liberty of the Earl of Meath, all of whom had Wicklow roots and who had come to the city in search of work.

We had country cousins in Wicklow, and when they made a trip to Dublin they always brought a half sack of potatoes or strapped an egg-box with a dozen eggs to their cases for Peg in Dublin. There was always a special smell from these egg-boxes, a mixture of turf-smoke, farm manure and the musty smell of hens' feathers. Sometimes the eggs were greased with yellow, salty butter, but more often they were packed straight from the hen, fluff and hen-dirt sticking to the rough shells.

For my mother it was important to know where the eggs came from, just as she liked to know which farm supplied our milk. We bought our loose milk from Mr Joyce's farm on the outskirts of Dolphin's Barn, and Great-aunt Anne Jordan's house and yard in Thomas Court Bawn in the heart of the Liberties could be relied on for the odd dozen eggs or the much-sought-after bluey-green duck eggs which my father had loved, but which were too strong for everybody else's digestion.

The business of sourcing fresh country produce was peculiar to my mother because she came from country stock, but a network of information regarding all black-market items such as tea and brown sugar, scarce sultanas, raisins and all other dried fruit was established through the years of the Emergency, and stood all housewives in good stead. Information was passed by word of mouth and the whole community benefited from the sharing. It was like the little rhyme we had learned in primary school: 'A woman said to me that a woman said to her, that she saw a women who saw a woman who heard a woman say . . .'

School for us had been with the Mercy Sisters at Weavers' Square on Cork Street, where we were cared for, watched over, disciplined and encouraged. Ours, we proudly boasted at *feiseanna* and competitions, was the best school in the city! My mother thought the world of the nuns and they of her, recognising an independent but reserved woman who had courage and resourcefulness when it concerned her home and her children. Our passport to the world of work was the primary school certificate which we took at twelve or thirteen years of age, but the nuns encouraged her and us to look beyond what was usually the end of formal education, for girls especially. For the boys who had been fortunate enough to attend a Christian Brothers

School, there was secondary education for those who wished to avail of it, though not every young lad did; nor were they encouraged to do so. Employment for young people never seemed to be a problem in the city, so that from a young age most knew exactly when and where they would earn their first wage.

Small factories flourished in the area, and word of mouth recommendation from a father or grandfather, uncle or aunt was usually enough to secure a job. Small dressmaking and tailoring shops vied with the bespoke tailors and the makers of Rialto serge, and the sawdust smell of the coffin-makers on Cork Street mingled with the nostril-tickling heat from the blacksmith's forge. The harness-makers on the corner of Bridgefoot Street gleamed with burnished brasses and glowing leather, and small shoe factories in the back streets competed with skilful craftsmen who worked in their own homes and had faithful clients who paid large sums for handmade shoes. Brass and iron foundries rumbled to the sound of hand-operated machines grinding and shaping raw metal and relentlessly stamping dies and moulds for every conceivable coupling, fitting and booming bell. Large, hard-pressed families were glad of their young sons' extra earning-power and hoped for better things when their boys would become apprentice fitters, electricians and plumbers.

Three laundries in the area, along with the biscuit, sweet and cake factories, swallowed up the female workers. And for those who didn't want to punch a clock and have their day dictated by the factory sirens, there were always the tiny shops: the pork butchers, the fishmongers, the beef butcher, the egg shop and vegetable shop, the fancy-sweet shop, the small drapers and the large drapers, where apprenticeships were bought and not within the purse of most families.

There were those of our friends with fathers in full-time employment with good firms in the city, who went on to private secondary education and schools of commercial training, but that was not an option for us. Madge and Babs left school at fourteen years of age and found employment, and my mother very quickly used the additional money they brought home to enrol them in evening classes. Babs' success in the Civil Service examination became a very big feather in my mother's cap, and she intended that I should follow the same path, but when my turn came to leave school I rebelled. Word of mouth secured a job as a tailor's assistant in a tiny shop, but I was soon bored silly with tidying, unpicking, noting measurements and sweeping up fluff and threads. I had a half-promise of a job in Wills & Company tobacco factory, which was equivalent to a young lad being offered a job in Guinness's Brewery, but the providential sighting of a scholarship advertised for the College of Commerce one evening when I was tidying the newspapers took me on a different path. My mother quickly realised the chance I was being offered; though the family would be deprived of my earning power for two years, it was the breaking of a mould. Now having spent scarcely seven months in my first job I was restless, anxious to move on again if I could, but wary of upsetting the apple-cart at home. Having seen my mother skimp to help me through two years of commercial college, the last thing I wanted to do was to cause her worry. But as I trudged wearily through December and into a new year, my own frustration began to surface.

'This paper is useless,' I muttered to myself as I scanned the advertisements in the *Evening Herald*, spread across the kitchen table. 'There's nothing in it.'

'Depends on what you're looking for,' my mother said crisply as she passed into the parlour with her coat on.

'There's nothing in the Situations Vacant column,' I answered, slapping the pages together and folding it carelessly.

'Oh,' my mother paused and retraced her steps. 'Who's looking for a situation?'

'I am,' I said gloomily, staring into the kitchen fire where the banked-up slack was slowly building into a great red mass. I itched to get my hand on the poker and bring the whole thing to life with one fierce jab. I had done it on a couple of occasions and watched the sparks burst and leap, incurring the wrath of my mother who had, she said, to 'kitchen' every bit of fuel she laid on the fire. I had suffered a long lecture on how all the city's fuel merchants had gone on strike and people were queuing for hours in cold, wet and windy weather to carry bags of wet turf home on their backs, and did I not know that fuel was rationed?

'Have you lost your job?' she said quietly. Realising just how quietly she had spoken, I jerked around.

'Of course I haven't lost my job!' My pride was hurt at the very thought that I would.

'Well, then,' she said, 'what's wrong?'

'I'm tired, I'm fed up and I've been sneezing all day.'

'I warned you,' she said, but decided against saying anything further. 'That paper's no good for advertisements; I'll get the *Evening Mail* on my way home from the Devotions, and I'll squeeze a lemon for a hot drink when I get back.' She was on her way to the Sacred Heart Devotions in Dolphin's Barn Church, so she jabbed her hat-pin into her everyday hat, pulled her coat-collar up and was gone. The two Aspros I took when she left had me half-asleep on the old leather sofa when she arrived home. I was beginning to regret having mentioned the Situations Vacant column, but my mother had the page opened almost before she had her hat off.

'What's wrong with your job?' she said, 'besides having to pay a handful of money for bus-fares to get there?' That was something I hadn't bargained for when I first opted to work in the countryside. 'We could always save for a bike,' my mother continued, 'but I wouldn't be happy with you cycling across that Naas Road, so I'm afraid that's that.'

'I like my job,' I said stoutly. 'I like the people. I know the work and I feel I'm doing well.'

'So what's eating at you?'

'It takes so long to get there and back and I'm rushing all the time to get to my Guide meetings in time. And I never get into town to see the shops – they're nearly closed by the time I get home on Saturdays.'

'Think of all the people who live in the country and only see the shops once in the blue moon,' my mother said under her breath, running her finger down the columns of ads.

'I'll have a look myself,' I said. 'I know what I'm looking for.'

'Do you?' she said, but her doubt turned to interest when I spotted that JC Parkes & Son Wholesale Merchants were looking for a shorthand-typist and that their offices and warehouse were on the Coombe. But there was an unforeseen obstacle in the way.

'No, no,' my mother shook her head dubiously. 'That's a Protestant firm. I can't see them taking a Catholic on the staff.'

'On the staff' in my mother's world meant working in a firm's offices, and Protestant firms of any standing rarely employed Catholic clerical staff. There had always been a strong divide between the Catholic and Protestant workforce in her day. Although the main employer in our area, Guinness's Brewery, had always employed a workforce of Catholic labourers, it had only in recent years opened the doors of its offices to Catholic white-collar workers; the new-comers were now usually the daughters and sons of existing staff employees and selected Catholic workmen.

'I can't see any difference,' I said to her, 'and what's more I'm going to have a try at this one.' The thought of her daughter applying to a sound Protestant firm for a good job as a shorthand-typist was something she had never dreamed of, though at least it banished the worries I knew she had had that I was dissatisfied with my new life as an office worker.

'Before you do that,' she said, 'what about trying for a Civil Service job like Babs? You could sit the next exam . . .'

'But I couldn't change jobs in the Civil Service when I felt like it,' I said.

'No, Miss, you could not, and maybe that'd be just as well. You don't want to be hopping from Billy to Jack.'

'Let's see how this Billy turns out before we think of Jack,' I said lightly, thankful that this new opportunity had presented itself.

When I was granted an interview, my mother was pleased, but still she worried that when they found out I was a Catholic they wouldn't give me the job. 'If they ask what religion I am, I will say it is none of their business,' I told her. 'It doesn't alter the fact that I am a good shorthand-typist and have seven months' experience behind me. That is all they want to know.'

I was proved right, and what was more, they offered me an increase of half-a-crown on my Killeen salary. My mother felt very proud.

'Always put a value on yourself,' we had been instructed when we were preparing for interviews. Industry was taking cautious steps forward after the end of the war; jobs were beginning to be plentiful, and I felt I was in a bargaining position.

'That was a bit risky,' my mother said when I told her.

'Jobs nearer the city pay more,' I informed her grandly. 'I told them that I was quite happy where I was and would only change for an increase in salary. And not a whiff of religion in sight. Mam,' I said, 'this is the middle of the twentieth century; we're moving on, not going backwards.'

Despite my airy remarks to my mother, from the very first day I was wary. Though my father had always taught us that there was no difference between any of us in the sight of the Lord, I was conscious that I had grown up somehow knowing that Protestants were different. I had no personal experience to guide me: I had no Protestant friends, and we had no Protestant neighbours. Protestants went to church and carried huge prayer-books, which could have been Bibles, though there was no way I could find out. Catholics had chapels and didn't have Bibles, unless you counted the Latin Mass-book which was used on the altar. Their churches seemed to be used only on Sundays, and even then they had only one or two 'services'. For the rest of the week the doors appeared to be locked, but again there was no way of knowing this for sure, because a Catholic would commit a mortal sin by attending a Protestant service.

Our chapels were always open and people were constantly streaming in and out through the doors, particularly in the city. In our own chapel in Donore Avenue we felt honoured to be part of a perpetual vigil of adoration in front of the high altar. A large roster hung in the porch for each day of the week, and we pencilled in our next allotted time when we completed our quarter of an hour, four people on separate prie-dieux in front of the high altar. Masses went on daily, and confessions, baptisms, funerals and weddings, not to mention novenas, rosaries and stations of the cross, kept the chapels open, warm and welcoming.

Short of asking each member of the staff their religion, I was almost certain that I would be the only Catholic working in the office. I went there with a feeling that I had to prove that I was as good, if not better, than any of the other girls, until I finally came to my senses and realised that religion was not going to influence how I dealt with invoices detailing so many dozen items of hardware that passed through the stores. It certainly didn't influence the kind and gentle Mr McMahon who was my immediate boss. He carefully steered me into the routine of the business and patiently sat on a high stool while he dictated letters, stopping regularly to check that I had got the names of places, addresses of firms and items to be dispatched clearly in my shorthand notebook. He had daughters my own age he told me, and he helped me settle and relax. Indeed nobody was stand-offish or toffee-nosed, but no matter how hard I tried I could not shake off the feeling of formality which I felt was always present. Everybody was vigilantly polite, so I tended to watch my p's and q's and certainly not shout and bang the typewriter when the tabulation key jammed.

There were five of us in the office, and we worked quietly and efficiently under a senior shorthand-typist, who announced some weeks after I arrived that she was leaving to take up a job as secretary to a well-known writer. She would take dictation from him and type his manuscripts in the seclusion and grandeur of his country estate. My mouth watered at the prospect. This was the stuff of romance: an office to oneself in a big country house listening to a book being created – how I wished I could find a job like that! She was excited about her new adventure, and as the front we maintained during those first months began to crack, I discovered a warm, generous nature who wanted to share her good fortune with us. This broke the barrier of reserve between us, which had nothing to do with whether we were Catholic or Protestant: a lot of it was simply due to the fact that it was an extremely busy firm dealing with clients throughout the country, so there was little time for chit-chat. Along with that, my social life outside the office was bound up with my Girl Guide activities; theirs was or seemed to be a continuation of Sunday church activities, so that they discussed flower festivals and the young girl who sang in the choir and who had a voice 'like the sound of a bell'.

As spring came round again and the weather was fine, I began to enjoy the fact that I was working within walking distance of home. I was no longer a child racing down Cork Street with an empty rexine shopping bag to queue for bread in the shop in Meath Street; nor could I dally on the way home with my best friend Jennie as we poked our noses round the door of the forge to watch the blacksmith grasp a horse's hoof between his knees and hammer on a new set of shoes.

'You're a young lady now with an important job,' I whispered to myself as I watched the stream of children heading up Ormond Street for my old school.

'You're now a young lady with her nose in the air,' I chastised myself as I side-stepped off the path straight into a puddle of water.

'Sorry, Miss,' from the Guinness drayman, busy loading barrels of porter through the trap-door in the path at the corner of Ardee Street, but that wouldn't compensate for the splashes on my new stockings. I made a mental note to walk on the opposite side when next I heard the Guinness drays coming along. Theirs was a distinctive, disciplined clip-clop, and the sound would reach me so that without turning I knew that one of the four-wheeled drays was just behind me. 'Horsey, horsey, don't you stop, just let your feet go clippety-clop,' I hummed to myself as they passed. Immaculately turned out by Richardson's carriers in Rialto, their drivers and helpers took immense pride in polishing the brasses and buffing the leather strappings on the horses. The blue and gold paintwork gleamed as they took to the city streets, and the men sat proudly in the apron-like protective clothing which they wore in summer; in winter they braved the wind and rain with frieze coats and bowler hats.

There were seven public houses on my way to Parkes and each one bottled its own porter from the barrels which were bundled into the cellars below the house. As children we had been hunted from the open holes in the pavements and I had shed many a tear when a halfpenny or a precious marble had rolled through the grating and landed with a plop on the barrels below.

'Mind the red raddle, Miss,' the drayman cautioned as I stepped back on the path again. It felt nice to be addressed as 'Miss', and he followed his remark with 'Watch for the hoppers, Miss, we've piled them around the corner.' Between the hoppers – hessian sacks filled with cork to cushion the barrels as they were bounced off the lorries – and the red raddle, a marking dye which fell like powder from the barrels, some mornings my journeys were fraught with dangers.

But the Guinness drays weren't the only threat to carefully polished shoes and pristine stockings. With his sacks of coal, turf and sticks, his iron weighing scales, and a brass bell ringing out to announce his arrival, the coalman was a menace, I decided in my best ladylike fashion, and I would nearly endanger life and limb to avoid him. Having negotiated the red raddle and the ropes and the hessian sacks, at the head of the Coombe I rounded the corner to be confronted by two black faces bejewelled with red-rimmed eyes.

'Mind the coal bags, Miss,' they chanted in unison.

A vigilant woman stood at her door counting the sacks they had slapped on the footpath.

'That's your five bags, Missus.'

'It doesn't look like five bags a' coal in the shed in there.'

'Count them, Missus. We brought five bags in.'

'That's all me eye and Johnny idle, let me tell ye.' She sniffed suspiciously as I cautiously stepped once again on to the narrow roadway. 'How do I know them bags were full?'

'You'll have to take our word for it, won't she, Jem?' And Jem shrugged his weary shoulders, tired from hoisting coal bags, and the dirty, coal-blacked sack slung across his shoulders to keep out rain and cold arched in a cowl behind his greasy cap, making him look like some mad mysterious monk. And was she prepared to take his word for it? I wondered as I looked back and caught the conspiratorial wink at Jem.

'Cowboys,' the woman muttered, certain that they had skived off the top of her five open bags to feather the nest of a sixth, one to take home or sell to the next customer.

'Cowboys,' my father used say generously, 'sure every profession has some.'

I had no sooner settled in my chair when Jack came in from the stores – or the stockrooms as they were sometimes called – with bundles of invoices which had to be recorded, tabulated and generally accounted for, and plonked the lot down on my desk. I had decided early on in my commercial career that I was never cut out to be a bookkeeper; nor was I the best tabulator in the typewriting business. Tabulating a long list of invoices and incorporating them in one single document, with numbers and names and prices strung across the sheet, was my personal nightmare. The longest line had to be added up, divided into sections and then margins set on the tabulator at the back of the typewriter, so that you typed the first part, banged the tabulator key and – hey presto – the machine sprang forward to the next spot. I found the theory slow to work in practice and decided, after long totting of letters and figures, that my eye was as good as any margin denominator. I gave up tabulating in favour of guessing, and found that it worked well enough.

Jack was older than most of us in the office. He had been with Parkes since he was a boy and had worked his way up through the system until he held a position of responsibility in the yard, but he was never quite 'on the staff'. He treated everybody with the same cheery informality when he breezed in with his brown shop-coat firmly closed to protect his clothes, and he was a mine of information about everything to do with the area.

'That's the old Weavers' Hall,' he said behind me as I turned from the big door of Parkes one day and paused to look at the empty niche above the door of what now appeared to be a woollen warehouse, across the street from the office.

'I know,' I said, 'but what did they do with the statue?'

'You remember the statue?' he said, turning to me in surprise.

'Well,' I said, 'I have a vague memory from when I was about six or seven of a curly-haired statue, with his hand outstretched. And I'm trying to remember . . .' I said. 'I think he had coloured clothes.'

'You have a good memory,' he said approvingly. 'You know, I thought as much. I said to the lads in the yard that times were changing when they took on a little Catholic girl to work in the office. A great firm this is, Miss, a wonderful firm to work for, and I should know it,' he finished proudly.

He nodded at the empty niche where pigeons were now perched.

'We'd a great day the day they took him down. The dealers around were sorry to see him go – poor old George II. He meant nothing to them, except that he was part of the old hall there, and it was a piece of Dublin most of them had grown up with. It was a landmark for them, just as the old hall had been for the weavers before them.'

'Why did they take it down, then?' I asked.

'Well,' said Jack, 'I overheard one old lady discussing it with another. "The oul' feet," she said sarcastically, "the oul' feet gev up on him – all the marchin' he had to do up there."

'"I never saw him marchin' down these streets," the other one said. "Who was he anyway?"

"'One of the kings.'"

"'Which one – the Wise Men or Herod?'"

"'No need to be sacriligious! Take care, the Lord's lookin' at ye.'"

Jack laughed. 'It was a lead statue,' he said, 'overlaid with gilt. It had to be removed. The lead in the ankles had rotted, and they were afraid poor old George would tumble down on some unfortunate passer-by.'

The Weavers' Hall had long since seen the last of its glory, too. Built in 1745 when the weaving trade was at its most prosperous and George was on the throne of England, it had been the brainchild of a French merchant, David Digges la Touche.

The weavers of broadcloth, or the woollen weavers, had been a part of the Coombe in the Liberty of St Thomas since the 1600s, when the Hugenot silk-weavers who had been driven out of France by religious persecution were given sanctuary by the Dean and Chapter of St Patrick's Cathedral around the corner from the Weavers' Hall, and allowed to set up their silk-weaving looms in the crypt of the cathedral. In a further burst of generosity the Dean gave them the use of St Mary's Chapel for services in French.

Jack's information set me walking one day around to St Patrick's, hoping I would get a glimpse inside. The threat of excommunication which was vaguely rumoured when I was in school to be the penalty for Catholics who strayed onto Protestant grounds was very much in my mind, and it stirred the thought that maybe I was now committing a venial sin by working for a Protestant firm. The thought got no house-room from me, however, and I knew I was not going to confess it to any priest: that would remain a matter between me and the Lord. I felt eminently sensible as I remembered the good twenty-five shillings I was earning each week from my Protestant firm.

In the Weavers' Hall which Jack and I now contemplated, they had formed a weavers' guild in line with the guilds of the barber-surgeons, the apothecaries, the cutlers, the painter-stainers and the stationers. Here the master weavers had assembled in their sober clothes and lain down the laws of the weaving trade. It must have been an important building in those days, I thought, imagining solemn men pontificating and adjudicating on the rules as to warp and weft, the proper quality of wool, poplin and linen, and imposing stringent fines on any who broke the rules. Cloth was referred to in warp – a strange name which no longer held sway. A five-dress warp was one hundred yards – twenty yards to the warp.

'Twenty yards to a dress in the old days,' I said to Babs as we struggled with four yards of material to make a full circular dress. She had enrolled on a dress-designing course and was busy instructing me on how to make a paper pattern.

'Who wants to drag that amount of material around? Think of the weight of it,' she said scathingly, 'and the washing!'

'Who says they washed them?' I said, 'they only hung them in cupboards and shook them out every so often. They probably only washed the hems after they had trailed in the mud.'

3

Poor People, Good People

JACK KNEW BY now that I was a child of the Liberties and a ready listener for his talk. He and I worked together regularly and, in between counting the invoices and checking the dockets, he would offer me little snippets of information about the history of the Liberties. Jack had lived all his life in Warrenmount, just behind the JC Parkes building.

'Warrenmount,' he said one day, 'was the residence of Nathanial Warren, high sheriff of Dublin one time.' Jack loved to come out with something like that, and he looked at me to see if he had my attention. 'His house was on the banks of the Poddle river – before they put it underground.' I nodded sagely, though I had no idea what a high sheriff did, or whether we had any in Dublin now.

'Was there a Smyley's school around here?' I asked him as we walked along the hall to the front door. I was still not sure of his religion, so I had to be careful not to call the school Protestant.

'Not that I know of,' he said, 'but above the road there, there was the Smith School – the Erasmus Smith School. Funny name that,' we agreed, 'Erasmus. 'Course that was one of the Protestant schools.' He indicated in a vague sort of way the buildings on the corner opposite Pidgeon's the pork butchers, where pigs' cheeks, pigs' feet, rashers, sausages and tripe were wedged together in the window. When we were small and any of us grumbled about school or the nuns, my father would threaten to send us to Mrs Smyley's Home, indicating the spot which Jack now pointed out as the Erasmus Smith School. I had a peculiar memory of the pressure of my father's hand when we used pass the building, almost as if he, too, was frightened that somebody might reach out and grab us from him.

'That school,' Jack continued, 'took in all the poor children from this area – all the Catholic children, remember, from around here. Now,' he said, 'that would have been sixty or maybe a hundred years ago. They taught the boys sewing and they gave them a meal in the morning and food to take home to their families in the evening.'

I phrased my next question carefully.

'When did the Holy Faiths come? You know, the nuns below there?'

'I was educated by them,' he said proudly, 'the best little bunch of teachers this side of the Liffey.'

'Hold on,' I said, relaxed now and bristling at the challenge to my own school above in Weavers' Square. 'I was with the Mercy's.'

'They did a good job on you then,' he said, 'fair play to them. But we had Padraig Pearse's sister Margaret in our school. Bet ye didn't know that.'

There was a lot more I didn't know and that Jack wasn't able to tell me, but I now had an adult library ticket which entitled me to consult some of the books which couldn't be taken out on loan. The upshot of my reading was that I became very glad I hadn't been born in the nineteenth century. It had been a time of dreadful poverty, hardship, privation and contagious illnesses. In their efforts to feed their hungry children, people took whatever hand-outs were available and, though proselytising was a regular companion to charity, they trusted in God to look the other way, for body and soul could not live together without food. Remembering the misgivings I had had about working for a Protestant firm, I felt I was on the side of the hard-pressed mothers and that possibly I would have done the same.

At work we never discussed the life outside our office in any great detail. There were occasional references to tea parties and church services; for my part I was very involved with my Girl Guide company and most of my evenings were spent at meetings or preparing badge-work, but nobody, I felt, would be remotely interested in any of those activities. Our great common concern was Victoria, whose budding romance was about to blossom, or so we hoped. On Thursday morning she arrived somewhat self-consciously at the office, and we noted her gleaming hair, tightly curled where it rested on her shoulders.

Victoria had a date once a week, and we basked in her preparations and wished her well as she took off, her golden hair carefully clipped in place, and on Friday we waited for the details of where she had been the night before. We were all with her in her ups and downs, and waited with bated breath for news of the engagement. Although I was conscious of the fact that I was working in one of the most historic parts of the city, and I was very curious about what had gone on hundreds of years before, this was now and life was very different.

Twentieth-century Dublin was what I saw every day through my office window. The street was never empty, never silent. Below my window shaggy cart-horses with low-slung drays and donkeys hauling tiny carts trundled by, carriers of anything anyone wanted. Weary old-young men pulled handcarts over the uneven cobbles. Bags of grain dribbled on to streets dirty with horse manure and slicks of oil from leaking buses, long past repair, but still in service due to the war. A young priest in his swinging cassock and jaunty biretta walked rapidly from saying a funeral Mass in Francis Street and on to his next visit at the Coombe Hospital. Long rows of cabs and carriages clip-clopped in uneasy rhythm from Francis Street or Meath Street chapels as they followed the funeral hearse to Mount Jerome Cemetery, while black-clad, white-faced figures sat upright on inadequately padded seats and stared fixedly at those who stood and blessed themselves as the cortège passed by. My mind drifted away from my work, imagining the scene at the hazard outside the chapel gate.

'How many can your cab take, Mister?'

The cab-man would drive the best bargain he could. 'How many are ye?'

'Well, there's Hannah and me and her fella, and the babby 'cos there's no wan to mind it. And there's me own fella, gosterin' over there as usual.'

'Half-a-crown for the lot of ye.'

'Count yourself lucky to get a silver florin. There ye are. Sure ye'd never think of chargin' for the babby.'

Messenger-boys with name-plated carriers whistled tunelessly as they manoeuvred their laden bicycles in and out of the slow-moving traffic, holding on to the backs of drays, causing unwary pedestrians heart attacks as they suddenly changed direction to take advantage of an empty bit of tow-path – then harangued whoever had caused them to swerve and upend their precious load into a crowded roadway. But everybody helped retrieve the books or the wallpaper or the groceries and dusted the young boys off, shook hands, doffed their caps and bobbed back to whatever they had been doing before the rumpus began.

The sound of children running from school, shouting to one another as they dodged in and out behind horse-and-carts, signalled our afternoon teabreak. As the street settled down for the afternoon, people put their heads in their neighbour's door to ask if anything was needed in Meath Street or Thomas Street, and would Mary or Maggie keep an eye on the children when they got back from school. On sunny days the kitchen chair was placed outside the window for Granny or Grandad to sit and take their ease and rock the baby in the pram, retrieve the soother from the path and prop the bottle full of milky tea on the baby's pillow so that the child could get on with the job of feeding himself, while the old folk blessed the fine weather and all around them and settled for forty winks.

Yet though times were changing, in many ways the conditions I saw on the streets were all too reminiscent of the conditions I read about from the last century. Nobody in the office ever referred to the poverty which was evident on the streets around us, and no beggars ever came to our big green door. It was as if we were insulated from the life teeming outside. And then I realised that I was the only one of the team who knew the streets of the Liberties and walked its ways.

Like my sisters and all the girls my age, I had joined the Children of Mary after leaving school and one Sunday evening when Madge and Babs had gone to Wicklow for a week's holiday, I attended our Children of Mary meeting on my own. I was asked by one of the nuns to deliver a parcel to a poor family she had been visiting.

'Don't lose yourself in the house,' she said as she gave me directions to a building in Chamber Street directly opposite my old school gate. 'They are big old Hugenot houses,' she said, 'and there are four families living on the ground floor. Be sure you bring the parcel to the right one. The mother has just had a new baby and she needs all the help she can get.'

From the time I turned the corner of the street until I reached the open hallway, I had a retinue of bare-footed hangers-on, eager to show me the way and curious to know what the stranger wanted.

'Who're ye lookin' for, Missus?' a small, freckle-faced boy wanted to know.

'She's not goin' to tell ye, are ye, Missus? What's in the parcel, Missus? I'll carry it for ye.'

'Don't mind him, Missus,' freckle-face said, rounding on his friend. 'Leave the woman alone, ye melodeon legs. I know where he'll carry it,' he said to me. 'Around the corner and you'll never see hair nor tail of him again.' He followed beside me while I walked the short way to the house. 'I'll show you where to go. It must be old Mr Bolger you're lookin' for, is it? He's been poorly.' But this 'Missus' of seventeen years was well able to look after herself and find the family she was looking for, and I shooed my attendants out the hall door of the tenement.

The door was opened to my knock by a fragile girl, whose face was drained of colour. Her hair hung limply on her shoulders. I was shocked to think that she didn't look much older than me, but she must be, I thought: two small children with bare bottoms and no shoes pulled at her skirt. I was completely unprepared for the stench that hit me. I swallowed hard and smiled as I handed over Sister John's parcel. Behind her I could see an open fire with an enormous clothes-horse standing in front of it, laden with uneven strips of cloth from which a soft steam was rising.

'Baby cloths,' Sister John explained when I reported back. 'They're just bits of sheets and old underwear that they use for nappies. God love the poor creature, but she wouldn't have the time nor the energy to wash them, so they're dried at the fire as they come off the child. That's why most of the babies run around, even in the coldest weather, with bare bottoms. Their little buttocks get very sore.'

I looked at Sister John, a gentle, soft-voiced nun from somewhere in Clare. She was, I knew, a choir-nun, one who had brought a substantial dowry with her on entering the convent. Sister John would have come from a comfortable family and I imagined she was not used to the hardship she now saw around her. I marvelled at the courage and stamina which sent her forth each day to teach in these hovels and offer help and succour when her day's teaching was done. It took courage and concern of the highest order to pin up her skirts, don her checked apron and plunge her hands into washing which was not her own, because the Sisters of Mercy were not just teachers: we saw them every day, walking in pairs, their gloved hands clutching black sack-like bags as they visited the homes of the sick and the poor.

Nuns had come to the Coombe in the previous century to work to draw the people away from the Protestant denominated schools. Proselytising had been inevitable in the early schools, and the poor neither understood nor cared when the bellies of their children rumbled. Dr Murray, the Catholic archbishop of Dublin, moved to influence what was happening, and began to involve the religious orders in the care and education of the poor.

Although they had no accommodation in the area to use as a convent, the Sisters of the Holy Faith had a small building in Westpark Street near Francis Street where they housed, fed and educated the children. They themselves walked each day from their mother house in Glasnevin and back in the evenings when their work for the children had finished. On Saturdays they gathered the boys together and taught them pants-making. I chuckled to myself when I heard this, having spent the first six months of my working life as a tailor's assistant where all the staff were young men.

The nuns had hot mugs of cocoa ready in the morning for the cold, barefoot children, and every child was sent home with a quarter of a loaf in the evening. The bakery shops of Boland's and Kennedy's supplied the nuns with the remains and more of each day's baking, and I looked with new respect at Gorevan's of Camden Street, a popular drapery shop; they helped many children with new clothes for Holy Communion and Confirmation days and shod many a chilblained foot.

'Did that brass plate on your school door never worry you?' I asked Jack.

'Which brass plate?' he said.

It said 'School for Young Ladies' and was polished every day.

'You know,' he said, 'I never noticed it until latter years. We went in the big green gate and never worried about what went on elsewhere.' But the brass plate had always irked me as I passed up and down the street. The convent for the nuns had been eventually built from the subscriptions of affluent Catholic tradesmen. Small trades flourished in the area and they gave generously to help the hopelessly large families of the poor; they gave too because the good health of the poor held at bay a return of the terrible epidemics which the area had suffered. And so the School for Young Ladies, while catering for the daughters of the affluent tradesmen, charged them high fees, thus funding the National School which now flourished.

The Sisters of Mercy had come at this time too. A Carmelite priest, Dr Spratt, had seen the need for a night refuge for homeless girls, and with the aid of the Sisters of Mercy he converted the old weaver's tenterhouse on Cork Street and word was spread through the streets of the city. Even now, as the Angelus bell tolled each evening, these sad women and girls could be seen making their way through a side convent-gate for their night-time's rest and a hot meal from the convent kitchens.

The Sisters of Mercy also founded a primary school in Weavers' Square, but ran into difficulties trying to maintain both the night refuge and the school. The archbishop advised them to apply for a government grant. I was rather sad to discover that my school had had to take the king's shilling, as I now thought of it, and suffer the attendant humiliations.

I had often wondered when I was a child about the little wooden altars which looked down on each classroom. A statue of the Sacred Heart or the Virgin Mary stood in each niche, on each side of which was a shutter. Nobody had ever explained to me the reason for the shutters, though I had wondered aloud many times as we took it in turns to empty jam-jars or vases and refill them with flowers. Now I knew. Under government rules no statue must be displayed in school-rooms except during the half an hour set aside for religious teaching.

'Oh yeah,' Jack said to me, 'nobody wants to talk about it. But I knew somebody who went there and she remembers it all very well. There was a notice on every classroom door which showed the time of the "half-hour". And on some days,' he said, 'these coincided with the lunch-hour.'

I mentioned it to my mother when I returned home that evening.

'Are you sure he's not making it all up?' she said.

'No,' I said, 'I did find a lot of things in the library – no, I think it happened.'

'It's a long time ago now,' my mother said reflectively, 'and things get a big hazy, but when I went to School Street School, there was no religion taught there. Before I went there, people talked about the teachers reading the Bible, but I never knew for certain. I do know, though, that we did attend religion classes in Meath Street Chapel every Sunday morning. The priests made sure we all attended and they prepared us for the sacraments.'

There was one person who might know, and I sought her out when next I attended the Children of Mary Sodality in the Convent Chapel. Old Sister Margaret I remembered from when I was sent to take messages to the convent as a child. She was old and bent and frail, but her eyes were like two bright buttons still and her mind was clear as a bell.

'Child,' she said to me as she grasped my arm tightly and propelled me to the convent door, 'those things happened and they did no credit to those who enforced the rules. We couldn't have survived without that government grant, and we agreed to abide by their conditions. There was worse than that,' she said, poking me in the ribs, 'the children were not allowed to call us "Sister". All the nuns were addressed as "Mrs."' She could see the shock on my face.

'Oh, it wasn't for long,' she said, 'and we all survived. Survival was the thing in those days,' she went on in a perky tone, 'and people were taught to overcome hardships. And times have changed and for the better, so stop taking everything to heart. For God's sake, girl,' she said, 'you've your life in front of you. Look to the future. Now that this terrible war is over, we can all start over again. Go on, child,' she said, 'and may God go with you.'

But I couldn't quite put these things out of my mind. As a child I had hurried on many occasions past the grey old building of the Coombe Lying-in Hospital, hardly giving it a thought, weaving my way quickly through the go-carts, prams, mothers and small children on the footpaths around. The name chiselled over the door held no significance for me then, but I now knew that a 'lying-in hospital' was a maternity hospital, and the name related to the fact that women who had babies were 'lying-in' for nine days after their baby was born. I remembered when Nance, our youngest sister, was born. She was born at home with a local midwife in attendance, and my mother was not allowed to leave her bed for the period of her 'lying-in'. Each one of us was a home birth, with my mother's cousins and neighbours supporting her, though I knew that at some stage my mother had attended the Coombe Lying-in Hospital for care after the births.

The hospital stood on the corner of Brabazon Row and faced directly on to the Coombe, dominating the street at that point. Steps from the front door curved down on each side, and children chased each other up and down while mothers and visitors sat and talked on the cold granite steps, their prams and go-carts lined up along the railings. Older children minded their baby brothers or sisters while mothers streamed in through the side gate of the hospital to the cold, stone-floored clinics beyond the yard. No children were allowed beyond the side gate and all children, save the new-born babies, were banished by the porter in his sentry-box, to await a mother's return.

'The risk of infection to a new baby is too great.' Dora, who was my mother's first cousin and had done some nursing in England during the war, was our authority on hospitals. 'Think of it,' she said, 'all those sticky, chocolate-streaked youngsters trying to kiss their new baby. No,' she said briskly, 'keep them out at all cost.'

'It's just so funny,' I said, 'that a hospital which produces the babies then has strict rules banning them from inside the doors.'

'The babies aren't the only ones to protect; most of the mothers in there need a well-earned rest and that's the only time they get one.' She shook her head sadly when I asked her about the black hearses I saw two and sometimes three times a week. Now, watching as I passed and understanding what was taking place in the big old grey building, the desolation of the little groups, clinging together in tearful disbelief as they walked behind a polished coffin, was the saddest sight of all. I tried to imagine the tragedy of a young father left to care for three or four or more young children, while a funeral hearse slowly took their mother to her final resting-place.

'You take too many things to heart,' Dora jollied me along. 'That's life, and think of the new life every day in that hospital. Mothers don't die all the time,' she said; 'childbirth is a normal, natural thing, and the care of mothers is getting better all the time. By the time you're ready, my girl,' she finished cheerfully, 'things will have improved a hundredfold.'

Facing the Coombe Hospital was a tall narrow house set among the many huxter shops on that side of the street. It was called the Gordon Baby Club and mothers and children trailed across to it from the hospital. It had been founded by Lady Aberdeen and was now run by fashionably dressed ladies who welcomed the struggling little groups. I couldn't quite put my finger on why I didn't like the look and the sound of that club. The ladies in their tweed skirts and velour hats were doing great work for the poor of the area; they helped the struggling women with their problems and sought to educate them in crafts. Maybe, I thought to myself, this is what I object to. None of these poor women have time to indulge them-selves in the luxury of crafts such as embroidery or lace-making. Or perhaps it was the fête they held in Lord Iveagh's grounds on the Crumlin Road which bothered me. They organised maypoles and Morris dancing and sports which were foreign to most of the children they were trying to help. It was, I argued, proselytising of a different nature and it made me uneasy.

Close to the hospital and the Gordon Baby Club was the kind of life which the well-meaning ladies hoped to wean the mothers from. All around the Coombe tiny huxster shops, dimly-lit with oil or gas-light, their doors scarred and broken, sat unsteadily side by side. Their tiny four- or six-paned windows gave a glimpse of their wares: bars of Fry's chocolate and Sunlight soap, lucky-bags and boxes of 'cough-no-mores', all arranged higgledy piggledy on an oil-cloth board. Tea in two-ounce or four-ounce packets stood on shelves inside, while turnips, potatoes, cabbage and white parsnips were spread on the narrow pavement.

'Can I have two ounces of Lyon's tea and a turnover, and me Mammy says will ye give her a half-pound of the broken biscuits, and could ye give her the big bits please.'

I had needed a small notebook for Guide notes and I took my turn behind a small girl in the tiny shop near the entrance to the old Widows' Home. In the dim light of the shop I had already knocked against the shiny scuttle which was used for measuring coal and potatoes, and in my stumbling I had also succeeded in knocking over the brass weights on the iron weighing-scales.

'And me Mammy says could ye put it on the book.'

The request was a statement rather than a question from the tiny figure at my side, and she smiled timidly at me. But the shopkeeper treated her smile with disdain. She ambled over to a drawer and pulled out a selection of grubby notebooks, poring through them carefully until she found the last entry.

'Tell yer Mammy from me that she paid me nothin' off the book last week. And she'll not get the whisper of a biscuit from me until she pays this week. Have ye got that?' The smile faded from the little face. The shopkeeper nonetheless handed over the items, replaced the notebook in which she noted the new purchases, and slammed the drawer shut.

'Ye'd think I was runnin' a charity in here,' she grumbled to herself as she wiped her hands on her apron. 'And what can I do for you, luv?' I felt guilty at having knocked over the brass weights and sorry that my purchase wasn't going to increase her prosperity as I handed over my two pennies.

Most of the huxter shops ran 'books' for their customers who bought most of their goods 'on tick'. The customer was then beholden to the shopkeeper, and more often than not there was very little chance of ever clearing the debt. It became so easy for a harassed mother to run a small child to the shop to add another item to the book. For many people this was a way of life – constantly living in debt. Some 'books' were never cleared. Pressure from the shopkeeper, as I had just seen, resulted in something being paid off when money came from a husband's Relief money or the Saint Vincent de Paul man gave a hand-out. For the shopkeeper, it was just their way of trading. When sickness or tragedy struck, they were the first to extend credit, knowing they might have to suffer the consequences, and often they would generously throw a parcel of groceries in a destitute customer's way. But there were no cheap bargains in these huxter shops: everything was full price or maybe an extra halfpenny or penny over the odds, and though the poor might always be with us, the shopkeeper kept her finger firmly on her profit.

4

Be Prepared

I WAS BEGINNING to find my feet at JC Parkes and enjoying the
relative freedom of working close to home and having time to
myself in the evenings, and I was seriously considering resigning
from my Girl Guide company. I felt the time was ripe for moving on
to something else, but I wasn't quite sure what that would be.

As a past pupil of the College of Commerce I was still involved
with the drama group there and went to the Abbey Theatre to see
every new production. This was one of the highlights of my life. I
followed the career of Ray McAnally, a civil servant who was the
golden boy of all the girls who worked in the GPO, marvelling at his
courage in making the transition from office worker to full-time
Abbey actor. I was so affected by Maire Ní Dhomhnaill's performance as the possessed girl in *The Righteous are Bold* that for weeks
afterwards I examined my every wayward thought for fear that the
devil might be taking possession of me.

A prize-winning performance by our group at the Dublin *Feis* in
Marlboro' Street, when Ronnie Masterson and I acted out a dialogue
between a cheeky maid and a haughty mistress in Irish, set my
thoughts drifting towards drama again. But a call to responsibility
from the Girl Guides came just in the nick of time, and my mother
never knew how close we had come to a crisis between the good
steady job and the glamour of the greasepaint.

'You're wanted in the commissioners' room,' the captain greeted
me when I arrived at the weekly meeting. She could see the surprise
on my face: a summons to appear before a commissioner was unusual.
'You've done nothing wrong,' she reassured me. 'Just hop along.'

'We need an assistant captain in Buíon Loreto,' the secretary commissioner said when I had knocked on the door and positioned myself at the end of the table.

'I'm too young to be an assistant captain,' I said. 'I'm not eighteen yet.'

'We know that,' she said, 'but we'd like you to help out. It's not easy to get officers to take on companies at the moment. The company is in need of an assistant captain.' She hesitated. 'I might add,' she said, 'that there are nights when you may have to take the responsibility of the company on your own – some evenings the captain has to work late.'

My career in the Guides had started about five years before as a result of my mother's determination that time was never going to hang on our hands. Madge was already involved with collecting for the foreign missions of the Holy Ghost Fathers and Babs had been recruited into the Legion of Mary. Her apostolic spirit soon dragged her three next youngest sisters into a junior praesidium, and the legion meetings in Bishop Street beside the big Jacob's chocolate and biscuit factory soon became a social outing as we in turn recruited more of our schoolfriends. Words like praesidium, concillium and curia sounded important, and when it was explained to me that these all stemmed from the Roman Empire and the Roman army, I conjured up romantic military scenes with men in robes and winding turbans marching through the desert behind a flowing banner, and I became proud to be part of an army dedicated to the Mother of God.

There were times when we must have sorely tried the patience of the very gentle lady who was our president, as we mumbled through the Rosary and the special legion prayers, trying surreptiously to blow out the candles around the statue and giggling at each other's reports. It was the reports which got to me in the long run. As juniors we weren't allowed visit hospitals or dead-houses unless in the company of an intermediate member, and though myself and Jennie, who had been all the way through school with me, had blessed many a corpse whenever we saw a black crêpe on a hall-door, most of our reports ended lamely with, 'went for the messages and helped at home'. As I had been doing that for as long as I could remember, I wasn't quite sure how it was helping the Mother of God's legion now.

'Can I join the Girl Guides?' I sprang the question on my mother as she was measuring the spoon-backed chair in the living-room to make a cover to match the new curtains she had hung that morning.

'No,' she said, her mouth full of pins. 'I know nothing about the Girl Guides and anyway it's very expensive to join.'

'It's only threepence a week.'

'The answer is still "no".' I was curled up on the brown leather sofa under the kitchen window, watching her as she planned and plotted the new chair-covers.

'Hold this pleat for me like a good child.' I squatted down beside her. 'Who goes to the Guides?' She carried the cover to the sewing machine in the corner and spun the wheel at the side. She was softening, I crowed to myself as I settled back on the sofa.

'Lots of girls from school have joined.' 'Lots' was three from my class and two from my sister Betty's. I mentioned their names. My mother knew their mothers well and approved of the families. I knew this was going through her mind and I hugged my knees tighter.

'Where are the meetings held?' I told her. 'Is it near the Scouts' place?' she ventured after a long pause, and I knew it wasn't the distance which was worrying her.

'Of course not – they're somewhere in the city.'

My mother pulled her sewing box close to her and turned her attention to sewing patent fasteners to the chair-cover and fixing the little pieces of tape for tying. Later that evening, however, there were quiet discussion with two older sisters which went into a hush whenever I was within earshot. I knew that Boy Scouts and their kin to Girl Guides was a big obstacle. The decision came on Friday.

'You can join tomorrow, but you've got to bring Betty and Tess with you.' That would be no problem. Betty and Tess would want to be with their own friends; that was the unwritten law of sisterhood from our first days at school, though quickly broken in times of distress when everybody rushed to the rescue.

Saturday afternoons and Sundays had never been the same for all three of us after that. My mother complained that she rarely saw us, we were so busy doing tests, tying knots, and reciting promises and prayers. However, her fears about the Boy Scouts receded into the background.

We did come up against the Boy Scouts, of course, but it was mostly at church parades and May processions and we stuck our noses in the air and treated them with the disdain reserved for a rival organisation, a male one at that. We never won out on these occasions. Every Sunday in May the whole parish was expected to turn out for a procession venerating the Blessed Virgin Mary, whose statue was borne high on the shoulders of members of the men's sodality, and on the feast of Corpus Christi the Blessed Sacrament was carried in procession by the parish priest in his golden chasuble of weighty cloth.

'Men at the head of the procession,' boomed from the microphones outside the church, and the command was duly enforced by the stewards in their best suits and bandolier sashes who marshalled the throng into line. The men's sodality was followed by the young men's sodality and the boys' sodality; behind them came the altar boys in their red and white outfits, the biggest boy swinging the thurible while the others rang handbells. The voices of the choir soared from loudspeakers fixed the length of the route. The First Communicants from that year walked ahead of the priests, scattering newly-picked rose-petals from wicker baskets suspended from their wrists, and the other children followed behind, every girl wearing a veil, and her sodality sash draped round her Sunday-best dress.

Sandwiched between the children came us Girl Guides, resplendent in our brown uniforms with the company flag flanked by a colour party, and behind us marched the women's sodality. Bringing up the rear was the young women's sodality and the stray dogs and young urchins who seemed to belong to nobody.

The Boy Scouts had the best position of all. They stood with the St John's Ambulance men and the Knights of Malta holding the line of the procession, their long poles stretched between them – keeping guard. I liked their wide-brimmed hats which they wore straight across their foreheads on ceremonial occasions and other times casually swung on leather thongs down the back of their necks. They looked like Mounties in the films. We poked funny faces at them when we passed, and embarrassed them by staring at their knobbly knees.

Threepence each was what it cost to send us to the Guide meeting on a Saturday; for my mother that was the best part of a silver shilling all told. Of the threepence which was handed to us by our mothers on Saturday, twopence was for the company and a penny to our patrol leader for patrol funds, but a chip shop sat a little way beyond Leonard's Corner and wafted its tempting smells through its open door as we passed each Saturday, and one cold spring day the temptation was too great. By common consent we piled into the chip shop and squandered the company funds on juicy golden chips, savaging them as if we had never eaten the good dinners our mothers had given us two hours previously. We lived with the danger that somebody who knew us would spot us and report us to the nuns, our mothers or the Guide headquarters, strictly in that order, because eating chips on the street, indeed eating anything on the street, was forbidden unlady-like behaviour. We got away with it for three Saturdays running.

On the fourth Saturday the captain smelled a rat, aided no doubt by the greasy smell of chips.

'Those girls who have not paid their company funds, please see me after the meeting.' She ranged us in a semi-circle. 'I see each of your mothers had no change for the past four weeks?' she queried, consulting her notebook.

We owned up. There was no way out anyway. Telling a lie was against the Guide law and, on reflection, it was against one of the Ten Commandments too. We could take it or leave it, our captain said, and as none of us wanted to leave, we promised to obey the rules.

As I progressed through the ranks passing my tests became of great importance. I practised reef knots, clove hitch, fisherman's bend, sheepshank and sheet bend, and memorised how, when and where they would be useful. I whipped with coloured cord a length of rope to hang on my belt – to what purpose I would never know; I learned the promise, the Guide prayer, the anthem and the basic rules of first aid, and polished my shoes till my mother decided to hide the polish. In front of the mirror in the kitchen, I practised saluting with thumb and little finger crossed, and I loved the secret handclasp which we had in common with all other Scouting organisations:

given with the left hand, it was a recognition of our solidarity with our Guiding and Scouting brethren world-wide.

'Banóglaigh Caitliceach na hÉireann, Fairce Átha Cliath.' I was proud of that name and thought it sounded much better than 'Catholic Girl Guides of the Diocese of Dublin'. We were not to be confused with our Protestant brethren who followed the rule of Lord Baden Powell's Boy Scouts: the first Irish Girl Guides had been formed in the early 1930s, but in 1936 we became a distinct organisation under the auspices of the Archbishop of Dublin. The Baden Powell scouts wore brown or khaki and their girls wore blue; we simply reversed the colours to preserve our different identity. We were basically the same, but as young recruits, fervent in our loyalty to our Catholic tradition and upbringing, we preserved a distance from the Blues and rarely had any contact with them.

My proudest moment was the night of my enrolment. With my hand steady on the company flag, it was lowered in front of the white-covered altar in the meeting-room while the chaplain and both captains looked on. I steadied my quaking hand, shot my fingers up in salute and recited: 'On my honour and with the Grace of God I promise to do my best to serve God and Holy Church; to help my neighbour at all times and to obey the Guide Law.'

I stepped back as the chaplain blessed my badge and pinned it awkwardly to my tie, then turned and saluted my fellow Guides and recruits, who stood in serried rows, each patrol behind its leader.

Guiding, with the joys, the hikes, the campfires, the whistle-stopping disciplines, the rules, the parades, the compulsory inspections of person and uniform, the taboos and the friendships had become a reality. I was hooked.

The learning went on and the feeling of being part of a special organisation grew, though at times it became too much for my mother.

'Out!' she said. 'Outside the back door if you must blow those whistles, although God alone knows what the neighbours will think.' While the war was on I thought the learning of Morse code and semaphore was surely very important. I had visions of sending messages to people in distress telling them help was on the way, and I had romantic notions of sitting on the seashore at Bray or

Sandycove and being the first one to spot a cry for help from a sinking ship on the horizon. Semaphore was something we could do anywhere if we carried the little semaphore flags with us; I never had much time for Morse code – that needed sophisticated equipment for tapping out messages.

'We could go to the Phoenix Park and watch for Germans. You know, like hide and when they come down in their parachutes we could signal to the soldiers.' Betty and I were semaphoring to each other from opposite corners of the backyard.

'How do you know the Germans will land in the park?' she asked.

'Because they always make for open spaces so that the parachute has room to open, silly,' I said.

My mother appeared at the kitchen door.

'Who's filling your head with nonsense about secret messages and German soldiers?' she demanded. The flags dripped to our sides.

'I was only letting on, Mam,' I said, terrified that she would take it into her head to ban Girl Guides for ever.

'Between the whistles and the flags and the tapping on the window-sills, I'm not in my right mind these days,' she muttered to herself as she turned back in the kitchen door.

Oh well, I thought, so much for my contribution to keeping war away from our shores. Even though the war ended without much help from me, I loved that feeling of being one of a group which must be prepared to take on all-comers. I wasn't sure quite when I must stand up and 'Be Prepared', but I was ready anyway, and that was all that mattered.

Much as I felt about the rules of first aid which I took to heart and mind instantly, I liked the rule which told me to 'Keep Cool; Act Promptly'. It stood me in great stead on the telephone switch-board when I was first learning to operate one, where two hands were never enough as I juggled with the receiver and wound the handle, throwing switches and connecting and disconnecting disjointed conversations. Everything would be all right, I told myself, if I remained cool and ignored the roaring of, 'I was in the middle of an important conversation! Who cut me off?' And if my calmness failed me in those first couple of weeks, I acted promptly by aligning all the red and black switches and scuttling to the cloakroom . . .

'Will you do it for a trial period?' the voice at the head of the table in the commissioners' room brought me back from my reminiscence. 'They have their own meeting room; it's loaned to them by the parish priest over in Dolphin's Barn, and it's not far from your home.' It wasn't far at all. It was at the end of the Back of the Pipes and across the road from Miss Finn's shop. But I had no training as a captain, nothing to prepare me for the task of taking responsibility for about forty youngsters once a week. Their numbers were drawn from Crumlin, an area of new corporation houses extending from the Sundrive Road to Mount Argos on one side and the Crumlin Road on the other, and they ranged in age from eleven to within a year or two of my own age.

'It's a challenge,' my mother said. 'You're very young, but the responsibility won't do you any harm. You've been through your own company and you know what's expected. Besides,' she went on, 'it's not as if you have the full responsibility of running a company on your shoulders. You'll only be an assistant captain.' I was proud that I had been selected. Secretly I had been growing bored with my own company, and this was a step forward. There was nothing to lose by giving it a try.

I was glad to exchange the tie I had worn as an ordinary Girl Guide for a slim brown officer's tie. It was with a sense of relief that I abandoned the junior tie; originally designed as a kerchief to be used in emergencies, its primary purpose was lost somewhere as somebody decreed that it should be starched, twisted and folded into a diagonal wedge of cloth suspended from our necks, and was of no use except as decoration. I liked the look of my wide-brimmed felt hat, caught at the side with a *'Bí Ullamh'* badge. If and when I became captain I would wear a yellow cockade. For the present I wore a yellow lanyard hooked to my belt, and primped in the mirror more than once before I attended my first meeting.

My charges were an active, exuberant bunch who were not beyond greeting the arrival of their new assistant captain, raw and inexperienced as they well knew, with hoots of derision and a palpable desire to test me out. My new-found dignity and the knowledge that I would have to instil some discipline if things weren't to get out of hand were sorely tried in the weeks ahead. More often than not I was left to take the meetings on my own and arrange outside activities. Pressure of work was forcing a long-serving captain to consider her options. She had greeted my arrival with relief.

Taking parade each week meant inspecting everything from their fingernails to their shoelaces and the all-important brasses – the tiny trefoil badge perched on the tie and the cumbersome buckle of the leather belt. With military firmness, and not long out of the ranks, I took the inspection seriously, but in my rush to get home from my job in Parkes I didn't always have time to polish my own gear.

'When did you clean your brasses last?' I had stopped before one of the rebels who had a cocky tilt to her head. I had already crossed swords with her when she had presented on parade with non-regulation white socks, strictly and firmly forbidden.

'When did you last clean yours, Captain?' she asked in a loud voice which sent a ripple of suppressed giggles down the ranks. One long blast on my whistle and silence was restored.

'I am not on parade,' I thundered at her. 'You are,' and I fingered the less than shiny badge and brass buckle. 'These are a disgrace to any Guide uniform.'

'We ran out of Brasso in our house, Captain. But me Mam says she'll have some next week!'

'What's the use?' I said to my mother as I recounted the incident and we giggled about the cheeky answer. 'It shouldn't be about polishing brasses and straightening hats and covering notebooks. So long as they're clean and have their shoes polished and their fingernails clean, and don't look as if their uniforms have been dragged through a hedge backwards, I'm not going to worry.' In the following weeks I promoted my rebel to the rank of assistant patrol leader. I reckoned that a bit of responsibility, coupled with the cheeky streak, would do her a power of good, and in the months and years that followed I saw that my decision had been right.

5

The Long Days of Lent

'**D**ENS OF INIQUITY!' The force of the voice behind me on the bus nearly shot the *Readers Digest* out of my hand. I turned, startled in case she thought my book was offensive. The *Digest* was one piece of luxury I allowed myself and up till then I had never read anything about the devil in it. I loved the feel of its shiny cover each month and the feature they carried of extraordinary feats of courage from all over the world, and I saved the condensed book at the back of the *Digest* for reading in bed. My mother had installed lights above our beds as we got older. 'I might as well face up to the fact that I've got readers in the family,' she said. 'I don't want you all going blind trying to read by torches under the bedclothes.'

'Only the devil's children dance during Lent,' the strident voice continued, and I looked around to see a stout woman, who could do with a bit of Lenten fasting herself, shuffling into a seat.

'It's true for ye, ma'am,' the bus conductor assured her cheerfully, winking at my startled gaze. I settled myself back and wondered about the devil's children and where they went dancing. I hadn't yet started to go to dances, except for the occasional *céilí* run by the Legion of Mary in John's Lane Hall, and these stopped for the six and a half weeks of Lent. The devil's children, it seemed, had to take their cloven hooves into the city dance-halls if they wanted to step it out.

Ash Wednesday came just when it was needed. It followed in the wake of the Christmas festivities which went on long after the last jingling bell had sounded. There was always a hooley for the New

Year when everybody opened their doors on the stroke of midnight and called 'Happy New Year' across the street as the church bells began ringing and the foghorns sounded in Dublin Bay. January and February brought annual Guide parties for each company, and as an officer, invitations to swell the adult contingent were many. The round of parochial pantomines dragged endlessly on, and as young adults we were now beginning to acknowledge each other's birthdays and celebrate them with parties in each other's houses.

We may have approached Ash Wednesday with a sense of martyr-dom, but we knew very well that both body and soul could do with a good blast of deprivation. While we moaned at the six and a half weeks of physical and social starvation that lay ahead, we filed into church and patted ourselves proudly on the back as we rattled off a list of penances we felt compelled to make and which would no doubt do us good.

The church in Dolphin's Barn was always packed on that morning, men and women grasping lunch parcels and all hoping that one of the priests would come out before the eight o'clock Mass and give out the precious blessed ashes, so that they could go to work in peace with the sign of penance on their foreheads: no announcement was ever made as to when the ashes would be distributed, which made me rather angry. When the line formed there was much elbowing and pushing in the crowded church; women who could have waited until the workers had been attended to pushed ahead with opened prayer-books so that the priest would sprinkle a generous pinch of the slate-grey dust on to the pages. I often wondered, as I stood in line, who was waiting at home to receive the blessed ash: was it a sick old person unable to come to church anymore or a small baby whose eyes would blink when the holy dust was sprinkled on its forehead?

As I walked in the door of the office I paused to think that this was the first time any of my friends in Parkes would definitely know of my religion. I wondered if they received ashes too. I would have loved to discuss it. I knew that what they called the Easter festival was a big feast for them, though they didn't seem to have to go through the rigours of Lent as we did. But nobody batted an eyelid at the heavy black cross on my forehead and we said nothing about it. I refrained from washing my ashes off when I went home to lunch. I was proud of that mark, and there was also a smug feeling deep inside of me about giving up some small treats, like sweets and chocolates, or giving up sugar in my tea.

'Ye get it easy nowadays,' Jennie's granny had told us when we were children. 'In my day it was black tea – no milk and no sugar – and ye did without butter or jam on yer bread every Friday. The black fast we called it.' I was glad that the days of the black fast were gone. It was bad enough once you had made your First Holy Communion to have to fast on every Wednesday and Friday of Lent, forbidden to eat meat of any kind. Eggs and fish were the order of the day, or just a plate of mashed potato, butter and cabbage. Fasting meant one full meal and two collations, and the question of what a collation was came up every year and was debated with great fervour.

'A collation consists of two ounces of solid food.'

'But we don't have a weighing scales in our house.' Nobody had a weighing scales. Nobody needed them. My mother weighed flour in her hand and used her common sense to sort out these matters. She had no time for scruples, and reasoned that the Lord above in Heaven had something better to do than check how many ounces of food she doled out to her family.

'You can take two hours to eat your dinner in the middle of the day and during those two hours you can eat as much as you can or want to.' This information came from Ann, but we treated her remarks with a good deal of scepticism.

'I heard a priest say it once,' she insisted. 'He said that's what a full meal is: you can have soup and meat and potatoes and a pudding, and then a cup of tea and a piece of cake.' We all looked at her in silence, hardly believing what she was saying. Cake was a luxury in our houses and only put on the table at Christmas or for visitors.

But no matter what it was, you had to give up something. There had to be a sacrifice. Most people gave up sugar or tried to give up cigarettes, and some men could be persuaded to part with their precious pints of porter.

We were encouraged to attend daily Mass if we could. For the first few weeks of Lent crowds packed into the Lenten Masses, but they soon thinned out, leaving the mothers, the elderly and the unemployed to keep the flag flying. But if after the first few fervour-filled weeks people were inclined to slip back to their old routines, the announcement that the missioners were coming jolted us awake. There was a buzz of excitement when the mission tent made its appearance inside the railings of the church grounds, and people began to wonder what the preachers would be like.

The mission tent itself was as good as a stall in a sale of work. Packed under its canvas were rosary-beads of all shapes and sizes, dangling from the stalls in lengths of glass, glazed pottery and wood. Holy pictures were stacked neatly in cardboard boxes, prominence being given to the particular saint of the order of priests come to take up residence amongst us. Statues of every size and colour – if not creed – stood on the counter, the large ones at the back beside the thermos flasks of the stall-holders who stamped their feet and snuggled into huge overcoats and scarves. There were miraculous medals, scapular medals and Sacred Heart medals; brown scapulars, green scapulars and blue scapulars; and Agnus Dei badges for the cots and prams of the babies.

Copies of *The Imitation of Christ* by Thomas à Kempis, which would normally only be seen in the windows of Burns, Oates and Washbourne in D'Olier Street, were lauded by the missioners and nuns and were much sought after as presents for girls entering convents. Sunday missals, prayer-books for Mass and devotions and hymn-books in tooled leather covers were stacked in one corner.

'I saw the girl from O'Leary's shop looking at the *Daily Missal* in the mission tent,' Joan reported one evening as we trailed home from the evening sermon and devotions. 'She looks holy, doesn't she? Is she going to become a nun, do you think?'

'Does she have to look holy to become a nun?' Jennie said belligerently, and marched ahead of the rest of us. I didn't see much of Jennie these days. Both of us had gone our ways into different jobs, and I was very much bound up with my Guide company.

'What's wrong?' I said as I caught up with her.

'Nothing's wrong,' she said, staring straight ahead. Ann and Joan had stopped to argue about the girl from O'Leary's shop and they tried to draw Jennie and me into it.

'There's nobody but a nun would want to hawk the size of that missal to Mass,' Joan said spitefully.

'She's not becoming a nun,' Jennie said quietly. 'She's getting married in two years time. I know,' she said, 'because her mother is a friend of my mother's.'

'Maybe she was looking at it for a present for somebody who is thinking of becoming a nun?'

'Don't be such busybodies,' Jennie said, but we all agreed that we'd have a look at the *Daily Missal* and that it might prepare us for the sermon on vocations which was sure to be on the agenda during the mission. Jennie wasn't with us the following night when we sidled into the mission stall to inspect the missal's flimsy pages. The light of the tilly lamp which hung from the roof of the tent cast shadows all round and did nothing to enhance the long rigmarole of Latin texts and responses which none of us could understand. I hoped that nobody would ever think of giving me the *Daily Missal* as a present, although the notion of carrying it into Mass and causing heads to turn and tongues to wag appealed to me a lot. Jennie's absence continued to occupy my thoughts as I flicked through the spiritual bouquet cards which were sent as presents at Christmas, mostly to nuns or priests for a feast day or as a 'thank you' gift. The friends of the recipient were canvassed as to how many Hail Marys, Our Fathers, Glorias and aspirations they were prepared to offer.

'I haven't finished saying the last lot I promised,' Ann said ruefully. 'I'm not promising any more prayers to anybody, or I'll be on my knees for the next ten years.'

'Don't be stupid; you can say the prayers as you go along the street and count them on your fingers.' Joan had no time for the impracticality of seeking a church every time she made a commitment to a spiritual bouquet. Her suggestion wasn't a bad one and so we kept the arrears at bay as we mouthed and counted in as rapid a manner as was seemly, squeezing our eyes shut and tripping over footpaths in holy concentration. What the recipients of the spiritual bouquets did with the prayers we accumulated on their behalf we were never quite sure.

'It's just like the Holy Souls,' Ann said.

'What's like the Holy Souls – none of the people we're praying for are dead yet. And if we keep up all the prayers we're saying, it'll be a long time before anything goes wrong with any of them.'

51

'Well, I was told . . .' began Ann.

'Oh here we go again,' I said tiredly. 'Who told you?'

'Sister de Paul said it when we were in school!'

'How many years ago now? Anyway, what did she say?'

'She said if one Holy Soul gets too many prayers and Masses, more than they need, like, then it's passed on to the next Holy Soul in need.'

'Who passes it on?' I demanded.

'God and the angels in Heaven.' Ann was sticking to her guns.

'You're joking; you mean that, at seventeen years of age, you really believe they have a book in Heaven and that they write down all the prayers we've been rushing through?'

'They only let the good ones through.' Joan had suddenly decided she was on Ann's side and these were not things to be mocked.

The mission lasted for a fortnight. The first week was for the women and young girls, the second for the men, young and old. From the age of fourteen every young person was expected to attend. My mother was prepared to be lenient if we wanted to skip a night but she would take no excuse for the final exercise on the closing Sunday. Groups of women would be seen making their way to the church with an hour to spare, to get a seat by the pulpit, under the eye of the missioner and in full view of everybody else in the church. Late-comers pushed into already full seats or some who left things to the last minute were escorted to improvised bench-seating on the side-altars, to be stared at by the self-righteous for the whole ceremony. Condensation ran in rivers down the painted walls.

The men took the mission with calmness and resignation. The old-timers sat by the iron radiators along the walls, spread their handkerchiefs on the kneelers and rolled Rosary beads, heavy with weighty crucifixes, through their worn fingers. Young men accompanied their fathers or attended with their friends, and all had their hair slicked back with water or Brylcreem and their collars and ties set firmly in place. The men's attendance never came near that of the women's, and the church was always only three-quarters full until just before the jangle of the bells from the sacristy announced the arrival of a preacher onto the altar: then the hardened sinners took a last puff of their cigarettes, rubbed their hands, removed their hats or caps and sidled in to form a solid mass across the back of the church. They ignored the calling hands of the ushers and refused the offers to grace the seats on the altar.

Missioners came in pairs, a young priest and an older, more experienced man who had years of dealing with the 'hard cases' in the parish. The queue outside his confessional was usually the longer. Hardened sinners or those who only professed to be hardened sinners sat in rows after row, shuffling their feet as the queue shifted slowly along. The priests spent hours in the confessional, wrapped in heavy overcoats against the cold and damp, and later they visited the very sick and called on the known slackers to cajole or reason with them.

The parish basked in goodwill when the women's mission closed at 4 p.m. on Sunday afternoon. Hats which had been bought in anticipation of Easter made their first appearance, new light summer coats were taken out, and younger women paraded to the church in a sea of green, yellow, pinks, blues and purples: the older women retained their shiny black straws and their sombre greys and blacks. There was a heartiness about the singing on the final Sunday and we held our twenty-five per cent wax candles, purchased from the stall outside and lighted from a taper held by the altar boys, reciting firmly and in loud voices that we renounced the devil and all his works and pomps.

I giggled to myself as I remembered the story of one missioner who exhorted his congregation to shout their response. 'Louder,' he urged as each renunciation was made, and 'The Louser!' came in angry tones from one hard-of-hearing penitent in the pews. I reckoned that any devil with a titter of sense had himself well away by now from the blazing candles, the swinging thurible, the rising incense, the raising of our many voices and the promise of glory on the gold of the priest's vestments.

As we entered Holy Week, on Spy Wednesday the altar was stripped bare of all its decoration, the Blessed Sacrament removed, the red sanctuary light extinguished and the door of the tabernacle stood bleakly open: the re-enactment of the Passion had begun.

There was only one Mass said in every parish on Holy Thursday, a High Mass with all the splendour and ceremony that the church attached to the day when Christ created the Eucharist. On my first Holy Thursday in the working world, I arrived in the office without any breakfast and, as the day wore on, I was looking forward to the visitation of the seven chapels in the evening.

After Mass the priests proceeded to a side-altar in the church and placed the gold monstrance amidst a sea of flowers and candles there, to rest till midnight when the doors of the church were closed. 'Which was the best altar last year?' We huddled in a group, having paid our dues to our first port of call, Our Lady of Dolours in Dolphin's Barn. On this day we would gain indulgences in each church we visited.

'Is it a plenary or a partial indulgence we get?' Jennie wondered. Jennie had been keeping to herself a lot lately, and I was glad she was with us as we set out on our journey.

'Does it really matter?' I was getting tired of all the accounting, but Ann was insistent.

'Does three hundred days remission mean that a Holy Soul has three hundred days less in purgatory?' Ann had spotted a flaw in this equation. 'Because I remember a priest saying once in a sermon that they don't have days in Heaven like we have down here. So the three hundred days may mean something different in Heaven.'

'How would he know? He's not been to Heaven.' Joan was pragmatic as usual.

'Can't we just forget about all the counting; let's pretend they're all plenary indulgences – they wipe out everything.' I wasn't sure about that but I wasn't going to let all these spiritual sums spoil my enjoyment of the churches we planned to visit.

We joined the throng walking down Cork Street, making a detour to visit our old Mercy Convent at the end of the street where the satin draping the tiny altar created a rich and shimmering beauty in the light of the candles. There was absolute silence here; the nuns in their habits and choir cloaks kneeling in prayer and adoration restrained all unseemly 'oohing' and 'aahing' as we tip-toed in single file to the altar, genuflected on both knees and recited our indulgence prayers. There were five more churches to be done, and we walked purposefully on to the Coombe and up Meath Street. A carnival feeling hung in the air as people strolled along the footpaths and down the middle of the roads, chatting together as they walked and breaking off as an occasional motorcar honked its horn to forge a passage. Everyone was intent on the performance of their Holy Thursday duty and the enjoyment and company of the evening. People passed and repassed one another as they took their different routes through the lanes and side streets from Meath Street Church to the Augustinians in Thomas Street, on to Merchants' Quay, over to Church Street where the rival Franciscans were, down to the Carmelites in Whitefriars' Street, and the longer walk to the other Carmelites in Clarendon Street, which was a bit out of the way but worth the effort if we wanted to prolong the evening.

'It's all so dreamy,' Joan whispered as we sat together and stared at the splendour of the altar.

'It's enough to make you fall asleep,' I said, mesmerised by the display of candles and nightlights, and I rested my tired feet on the kneeler.

'Shsh,' came from a seat behind and heads turned to chide us for our irreverence. We stared solemnly ahead and pretended we hadn't spoken.

'Makes you feel really holy, doesn't it?' In the warmth and cosiness, with bowed heads all around me, I felt I could pray for the rest of my life. 'You could nearly think about becoming a nun if you stayed here long enough.'

'There's more to becoming a nun than sitting in a cosy chapel,' Jennie said sharply, and I looked sideways at her.

'I'm beginning to feel hungry,' I said. 'I wish all this fasting was over.' Tea had been a long time ago and the thought of a cup of black tea, because I had now given up milk, and two plain Marietta biscuits for supper, wasn't very satisfying.

'It's Holy Thursday, the night of the Last Supper,' my mother said when I got back, and she put out a plate of fairy cakes on the table. 'Our Lord and the twelve apostles had a big celebration that evening, so eat these now.'

At noon on Good Friday the wireless was switched off and the piano firmly locked. My mother sighed in the relief of silence as we all tried to observe and respect the three Hours of Agony. We mimed and pointed, spluttering and mimicking until the hands of the clock in the parlour sounded the chimes of three o'clock and our tongues were finally unlocked. And then it was Easter Sunday morning, and the church and chapel bells rang out with clarity and insistence. They clamoured over and over, and the Easter sun of the risen day streamed in through the stained-glass windows. At home our chocolate Easter eggs sat squarely in their boxes on the chiffonier in the spick-and-span parlour. The long days of Lent were over.

6

Wicklow

OUR FAMILY TREE was rooted deep in the soil of West Wicklow. My father was one of a family of seven sons and three daughters from the small hilly town of Tinahely where my Grandfather Crowley ran a small bakery; my mother was the only child of Johnny Whitty and Elizabeth O'Neill of Kyle, Ballinglen, who married and settled in Dublin where Grandfather Whitty was employed as a drayman with Guinness's Brewery. Our two 'aunts', Aunt Mary Keenan who lived in a small farm just above my great-grandfather's old home, and Aunt Nanny Keenan who lived at Three Wells above Aughrim, were really my mother's first cousins. They were married to two brothers, and most of our cousins were older than we were. The pull of Wicklow was immensely strong and drew us back year after year when the long summer holidays were upon us. This year I was going to go there on my own, on my first holiday from work.

That week of my adult holiday was a good one. I wandered on my own over the brow of the hill and along the back road to the town of Aughrim; I heard the swish, swish, swish of the narrow ribbon of milk as it hit the bottom of the can held between Uncle Dan's knees and I tried with inexperienced fingers to coax milk from Bessie the cow, who rolled frightened eyes at me as I sat unsteadily on the little three-cornered stool. I carried water from the only one of the Three Wells used for human consumption, dipping the bucket expertly into the cool recess, balancing it on the shiny flags, perpetually wet with water drawn for half a dozen homes, and leaning well to the right as I carried the bucket of sparkling water home to the house.

In the evenings when the cows had been milked and the fowl, the pigs and the calves had been fed and bedded and the fading day had yielded to the gentle night, Mary, Liam and I walked to the wells in our light shoes, the heavy working shoes discarded by the kitchen door. Neighbours gathered for a chat, to quietly discuss the day's doings and make plans for winter sowing, fencing, snagging turnips and dipping sheep. As the fat toads croaked in the damp growth beside the wells, we laughed and talked while the crickets chirped and the rabbits on the rise of the hill were etched against the lingering evening sky.

We had laid my father to rest the previous summer in the graveyard above Tinahely, and during the week in Aughrim I cycled with Liam the seven miles to Kyle to visit Aunt Mary and to take part in the preparations for the pattern, the annual ceremony of blessing the graves. After we cleaned and tidied the graves and I traced my father's name where it had been newly added to the gravestone of my grandparents, I sat back on my heels, closed my eyes and remembered. Every year we had gone back for the pattern, the annual ceremony of blessing the graves. The train from Dublin to Shillelagh left Westland Row at twenty-five to seven on the Sunday morning. With Madge and Babs in charge, Betty, Tess and I set out at twenty-five to six from our home. My father and mother, with Nance in the go-car, followed behind, giving us a five-minute start. Madge calculated that if we were at the Holy Faith Convent on the Coombe when their chapel bell called out the morning Angelus, then we would be in time for the train.

At Westland Row we sat on the station seats and drank milk from the bottles which my mother had packed at the back of Nance's go-car. I loved the hustle of the railway station, with trains shunting back and forth spewing cascades of steam and raining soft, insinuating coal-dust. I loved the sound of the guardsman's whistle clamped between his teeth, and watching the red flag raised in his hand as he waited for the latecomers rushing past the ticket-collector's hut. With pennies clutched in our hands we made for the name-plate machine where we punched our names and addresses onto pieces of tin. We swung the big iron handle through the letters of the alphabet, made mistakes, corrected them and swung again. As we waited for the train to Shillelagh we read aloud the captions under the huge advertisements; we laughed at the two faces of the Mac's Smile blades, and at the dopey man in the Andrews Liver Salts who searched through his case for the all-important tin which was peeping from the pocket of his sprawling posterior and who perplexedly mouthed the words, 'I must have left it behind.' And we always chanted the advertisement for the Waverly pen:

> 'It came as a boon and a blessing to men,
> Pickwick the Owl and the Waverly pen.'

From Westland Row to Woodenbridge we all dozed, waking in time to change trains to Kilcommon, below Funeral Hill, where we stumbled from the train to breathe good, fresh country air. The smell from turf-fires as the smoke rose lazily in the stillness of morning was like heady perfume for me. We were well in time for the second Mass, and then my mother and father spent the rest of the morning and early afternoon painting the kerbs of the family's graves while we helped pull weeds and water flowers. My great-grandmother's iron cross had been cast at the great Hammond Lane foundry in Dublin, and when we found it my mother would once again say, 'Your great-grandmother, God be good to her, she survived the Famine, you know.'

It was my father's pride to walk the street of his beloved home town and introduce his family to those he met, and our welcome was always warm and strong. Tired and happy with work well done, and the pattern for one more year dutifully attended to, and 'God bless' and 'God go with you' and 'God give you a safe journey home' echoing in our ears, we sat contentedly on the green garden benches of the little railway station, pictures of white-washed cottages and stacks of dark brown turf still fresh in our minds.

There had only ever been one exception to our summer routine, the year I was twelve years old and Tess was nine, and we had both been awarded scholarships to the Connemara Gaeltacht by the Irish Congress of Trade Unions. We were boarded in the home of Stiofán Ó Líodáin, *an táilliúr*, up a long narrow boreen bordered with grey walls made of stones culled from the surrounding land. After I had nearly drowned my younger sister as I attempted to wash her hair in a bucket of water, Bríd, who was the eldest daughter of the house and the apple of everybody's eye, kept a protective eye on both of us for the rest of the month and together we raced down to the sea to spend our days climbing rocky ledges, marvelling at the myriad colours of the tiny shells, bursting bubbles of seaweed and gathering carrageen moss.

But for the first week the days were long, as long as the stumbling boreens which drifted across a lonely landscape and hid the home-sickness which plagued me. Some of the *bean a' tí*, I always felt, weren't quite easy with the 'scheme' which scattered Dublin children over the townlands of Connemara, we to learn our native tongue and their homes to earn much-needed additional income. For our part we had to adjust to a very different way of life: the rapid-fire Irish of their intense conversation, the bare feet toughened by rough ground, the weather-beaten, salt-sprayed faces of the men. On Sundays we followed our *bean a' tí* to Mass and I watched fascinated as the brown Sunday shawls slipped from every grey head bent in prayer, while the rest of us sat suitably head-covered as Canon law decreed.

We improved our spoken Irish and tried to initiate my father into the mysteries of the language which he loved to hear us speak. He and my mother, who had no contact with us except by letter, were anxious to see us for just one visit to satisfy my mother that we were safe and well. They journeyed by train to Galway city, took a small rattling bus to Spiddal and walked the rest of the weary way to see us in Cor na Rón Lár.

'*Dia dhuit*,' we instructed my father was the customary salutation when you met somebody on the road. '*Dia's Muire dhuit*' was the response expected. But my father could not quite manage the response, so he proudly shouted '*Dia dhuit*' to everyone he met before they had a chance draw breath.

Many of my father's generation were gone now. I said goodbye to the home of Aunt Mary, a widow whose grown-up sons and daughters had all scattered. She was about to follow her family to Dublin, where her sons were employed by the Guinness Brewery. I wandered across the hill on my last day while Liam discussed business with Aunt Mary and his cousins. I looked across the valley to where Lugnaquilla stood hunched against a darkening sky, its broad shoulders heaving amid swirling summer mists. I wandered into Jack's corner where Aunt Mary had sown her kitchen garden and I sat once more on the hillside where my mother had played as a child. As I poked around in the ruins of my grandmother's house, a three-roomed cottage with a tiny loft, in my mind's eye I could see the photograph displayed on our parlour wall of an elegant woman with proud bearing, and I recalled the grandeur of the only other grand-aunt I had known, Aunt Biddy, with her lace petticoats and buttoned boots. I looked at the crumbling walls and the tiny garden and wondered from whence did the grandness of the seven daughters in my grandmother's family spring.

I rambled far that day and was saddened by the derelict houses I passed, homes which in my mother's youth would have been 'rambling' houses, where neighbours gathered in the evening to tell stories and make music; they stood now, monuments to an uneconomic farming period when doors were quietly locked and whole families disappeared from the land. Cousin Nanny of Kyle was Aunt Mary's daughter and the one who kept us in check when we were children. The fire which Nanny tended on the hearth, coaxing and hoarding it to bake her soda-breads in an iron pan slung over the glowing embers, would soon be extinguished.

While the others still chatted I made for the dairy which stood next to the parlour, dark in the side of the hill where it was shaded from the heat of the sun. The wooden barrel which was used for churning the butter stood there, scoured and scalded, and I remembered days when I had been allowed to turn the handle. The wooden clappers, lined and grooved for shaping the butter stood upright in the great earthenware jar. Nanny always knew when the butter was nearly ripe and she allowed us open the door of the barrel, lift the lid and test the yellow beadlets which floated to the top. Back in the house before we said our goodbyes, I ran the knife along the back of the lump of butter sitting on the table, and watched the beads of moisture springing to the surface.

And so the week had gone. Uncle Hugh Kenny, husband of another of my mother's first cousins, was escorting me back to Dublin. He was impatient with me as I bent to adjust the saddlebag on the back of my bicycle and sneak one last look up the shaly road to Three Wells. We had fifty miles to cycle before dark set in. The tyres were well pumped, a puncture repair outfit was in the back bag among my summer dresses, a pump set in readiness on the frame, and there was no further excuse to linger.

We passed through Glenealy where the sign at the end of the hill said, 'Steam locomotives not allowed.' In Ashford we stopped for a glass of fizzy lemonade and to eat the apple Aunt Nanny had given me. Uncle Hugh was a tower of strength and pushed me ahead of him, one hand on my shoulder, when I flagged. I was glad to recognise the Glen of the Downs, and when I caught sight of the familiar signs of Kilmacanogue and the Sugar Loaf mountain, I knew that Uncle Hugh's home in Dun Laoghaire wasn't too far away. After Aunt Bridgie had fed us bacon and eggs I was sent on my way, the thought of home lending the bicycle wings.

'Never again,' I said to my mother as I leant the bicycle under the window-sill at the top of the garden and eased my sore buttocks on to an easy chair.

'It was your choice,' she said as she placed a cup of milky tea in front of me and settled herself to hear all the gossip from the country; who was dead or dying, or who had been married or was still on the shelf. I wasn't much good to her. I had only listened with half an ear to tales of calamities, scandal and gossip, and I was so exhausted that my head lolled dangerously close to the hot teapot. She pushed me ahead of her up the stairs, waited while I undressed and lay flat on the bed, then gently eased my aching calves beneath the bedcovers and tip-toed from the room. The questions could wait for another day.

7

Invitation to Tea

THE LETTER WAS simple. 'Come to tea on Saturday,' it read, 'at about five o'clock. I've been hearing a lot about you and I would like to see you.' The letter was signed 'Angela Healy.'

I had never had a formal invitation like this before, and more than that, it came from one of my former teachers in the College of Commerce. My mother was as intrigued as I was. 'Wear your good tweed coat and the pill-box hat,' she advised. The tweed coat had initially belonged to her; after my father's death, when I was starting work, she had taken it to a tailor in Harold's Cross who remade it as a fashionable princess-style coat, nipped at the waist and flared to the hem. I wore it with a black star on the right elbow and a black blouse and skirt, to show that I was in mourning. 'You can borrow Madge's new white blouse,' my mother said; 'it'll start you in second mourning. It's about time we all put a bit of colour back in our clothes.' I was glad the period of mourning was coming to an end, and white, mauve and grey could be introduced for the last few months.

I looked at the letter again. 'Angela' – so that was her name. All our teachers were addressed as Miss or Mister. There was always giggling when we uncovered a Christian name, but Miss Healy had signed all roll-books and notebooks with a large 'A' and held her distance. The class loved her. Thin, with short bobbed hair, she walked gracefully, with her head a little sideways as if to note every puddle on the footpath and step around it. Her rule over our class was firm, and although she suffered the little tricks we played on her and listened to our chatter at the start of class, the moment she straightened her black academic cloak, looked at us over her glasses and said, 'Now girls,' we knew that we must come to order.

'A lovely name,' my mother said, 'but you surely won't call her that?' she continued anxiously. 'You'll still address her as "Miss"' won't you? After all, she was your teacher.'

My heart thumped in my chest as I knocked on the door of the two-storey house in Rathmines, where Miss Healy lived with her mother. Tea was always a formal meal: in our house it meant a table set with proper table settings. No matter how plain the fare, the ritual of sitting to the table to eat was important. Miss Healy waved me in to her living-room, where the table was elegantly laid with a white lace tablecloth, flower-patterned china and silver cruets beside the matching china sugar bowl and milk jug. The two-tiered cake plate was piled with maderia buns and slices of fruit-cake, and beside it lay matching napkin rings which held stiff white napkins.

My mother had taught us good table manners and how to behave in company, but still I wished myself miles away as I prepared to eat the plate of cold ham which was placed before me. I hated ham but managed to swallow it between little bites of thin bread and butter, while Miss Healy attended to her mother who sat in an armchair with a small table beside her. I ate like a bird, afraid to relax in case a crumb fell on the pink carpet at my feet; I wasn't sure if it would be good manners to pick it up and if I did, what I should do with it.

'You didn't last long in the country job,' Miss Healy chided gently as she poured first milk and then tea into the china cups.

'No,' I admitted, tongue-tied for the first time in my life.

'So the adventure wore off,' she said. 'They were anxious to keep you, you know. They were in touch with the school for a replacement and that crusty branch manager had no idea what office you had gone to.' I thought of the crusty branch manager; he had been decent enough after I had given my notice and made sure that I got proper holiday pay for the days I had worked, and he had given me a reference, though somewhat grudgingly. He never liked giving references, he said when I insisted; if people wanted to know, let them ring up: he hadn't time to be dictating rubbish.

I explained about my job in Parkes and as we talked she drew out of me my story of the distressing scenes of poverty I witnessed on my journey to and from the office.

'That can be very depressing,' she said and put like that I suddenly realised that, yes, the greyness and drabness of the area was getting to me. And I also felt a bit lonely there as it seemed unlikely that I would become good friends with any of the staff; we didn't have much in common besides our work.

'How would you like a job in town?' she said suddenly. She smiled as my head jerked up. 'I thought as much,' she said. 'I'm glad I wrote to you.'

'But I'm working with a very good firm,' I said, 'and I've only been there six months. It's not a typing pool,' I explained. 'I take dictation in shorthand and I'm getting a lot of experience.'

'Now,' she said, 'you remember Father Condren? He remembers you from religion class. This job is with a friend of his, who is the senior partner in a very old firm of solicitors.'

Of course I remembered Father Condren. When I had represented the school on the inter-technical schools quiz on radio, he had given me a special prize. 'You kept our end up,' he had said, as he passed the picture down the class to me. 'You didn't let me down.' I had been so proud. For two full days the two senior classes had sat in the college hall and written answers to questions fired at us from the podium, all of them in Irish. At the end of the second day they had eliminated all but two of us, Clare from Blanchardstown and myself, and one of us would now represent the college.

'She won't be home until late,' Jennie had told my mother as she handed over my files and textbooks.

'What's wrong – where is she?'

'She's gone to Radio Éireann,' Jennie replied, 'and if you turn on the wireless now, you'll probably hear her.' According to Jennie my mother had rushed to the radio in the corner, shouting: 'She's only got her everyday clothes on; she's not fit to be seen on the wireless!' I was in the studio in Henry Street facing a studious-looking boy from the north side of the city. We fought it out like Trojans until he made a slip. My next answer was the decider. In beautiful Irish from Máire Ní Ghrada came the question: 'Who said, "Am I my brother's keeper?"' I dithered as the seconds ticked away. Which of them was it? I thought as my mind raced over my religious knowledge, 'Cain and Abel were the sons of Adam and Eve . . .'

'Cain,' I spluttered just before the scorekeeper banged the gong. The honour of the college had been saved, and Father Condren had not forgotten it.

'He thinks you'll be suitable for the job,' Miss Healy said as I returned from my trip down memory lane. 'It's a very responsible position to work in a solicitor's office. They need somebody they can trust.'

'I'm not sure,' I began. 'My mother' – and I immediately knew I had my grown-up voice on when I hadn't referred to 'my Mammy' – 'My mother won't like to see me changing jobs again. She's very proud of where I am at the moment.'

'Throwing away a good job,' was how my mother reacted to the story I brought home. 'You won't get a chance to work with a firm like that again.' But the thought of a job in the city centre among the fashionable shops, with people on the streets who didn't look as if life were one long struggle, was making my mind up very quickly.

'I hate the thought of a good job like hers going out of the family,' I overheard my mother confide to Madge. 'I suppose they'd never give the job to Betty? She's just about finished her commercial course.' A week later I got the job in the solicitor's office and handed in my notice at Parkes.

'Can I have a reference please?' I asked the managing director. He nodded gravely. Encouraged by his courtesy I decided to take the plunge. 'I have a younger sister,' I said, 'who's just ready to leave commercial college. Can she be interviewed for my job?' He looked startled for a moment but recovered quickly and distantly he told me that he would consider it. That evening I told my mother, 'Betty has an interview for my job next week,' and I stressed the fact that there was no guarantee with it. But the managing director, a model of understatement in most circumstances, was better than his word, and the following week Betty got the job.

Grey-haired and slightly bent, in demeanour as benevolent as an ageing grandfather but strict and demanding in practice, my new employer, Mr George, explained as if to an eager child the legal work his firm was engaged in. He emphasised the strictures which would be imposed on me as to secrecy and confidentiality, and the courtesy which I would be expected to extend to all the firm's clients. He lectured me that the work I would now be doing would involve not mere paperwork but also personal contact with people who were important to the business. As he talked I wondered if he was going to swear me to some great oath of secrecy and I imagined I should reach out and touch one of the weighty tomes ranged behind his back and recreate my Guide promise in legal terms. But the solemnity of his words and the dull brown of his office began to envelop me, and I realised that flippancy held no place in the serious business of law. The window behind Mr George's desk was covered on the lower half of the sash with a yellowed masking sheet though it only looked on to the back of the buildings behind ours. This detail gave me much thought; more than anything else it emphasised for me the degree of discretion demanded in a solicitor's work.

The front office where I worked was on the first floor overlooking Fleet Street and the buzz of busy people reached up from the street below. Four of us shared the office with a switchboard, two overflowing filing cabinets and boxes of legal stationery. Miss Moore, the book-keeper, crept to the room above us which she shared with the In and Out journals, cost books, clients' ledgers, solicitors' ledgers and the rent accounts of country estates. The responsibility for the solvency of the firm seemed to rest on poor Miss Moore's shoulders, and at times she appeared to droop beneath the burden.

The ledgers were mighty foolscap tomes with red or green bound spines, and every morning tiny Miss Moore carried them from the safe in the corner and spread them out on her desk where they were solemnly consulted by the two partners. Miss Moore shyly skipped from book to book, explaining an entry here and double-entering an item there, laboriously copying figures or text in her beautifully clear handwriting. Those books were her children and she kept them in strict order. She hovered over me when I entered her sanctum, steering me through rent-books and gale-days, petty-cash items and matters for logging in preparation for bills of costs, and each evening she gathered the cumbersome ledgers in her arms, returned them to the safe and locked it carefully for the night.

Our office was open to the public. In my first few days I dreaded to see a client arrive at the long counter, and when they dinged the little handbell I would shrink behind my typewriter. Besides learning to deal with clients, some of whom could be extremely unpleasant if their solicitor was not there to deal with them on the spot, I now had to come to grips with the small switchboard which linked the different offices. As I was last in and by far the most junior of the staff, I was expected to jump every time the phone rang. My senior stood over me and thumped me on the shoulder if I forgot to press the holding key.

'First rule,' she would storm at me, 'press the holding key. It gives you time to think. Then press the extension key, and for God's sake don't let the client hear you talking. Mr George or Mr Gerard mightn't want to speak to them.' So I clanked the handle and waited while the solicitors took their time in answering. After a while I learned to keep ringing until they responded: if they were busy, so was I, and it was no use either of them trying to fool the rest of us who were trying to get on with our part of the business.

I had been engaged as an assistant to Mr George's secretary, who was beginning to find the volume of work too much for her. Mr Gerard, the junior partner, had his own secretary, a beautiful blonde girl with Veronica-Lake style hair falling over one eye which she carefully clipped back when the pressure was on and the typewriter had to fly.

They were as different as chalk and cheese, the two partners in the firm, and they were aided and abetted by a fledgling solicitor just out of his apprenticeship. The junior solicitor was responsible for the small amount of court work the firm was engaged in, the district court fines and appearances in the circuit court. We were basically a conveyancing firm, dealing with the buying and selling of property, and had been solicitors to old families for a very long time. I always got the impression that the partners didn't care much for the civil courts and never really encouraged that business. The young solicitor was tall and appeared to be perpetually falling over his long legs as he took the corridor to his tiny office in three strides, dashing up and down the stairs, in and out the front steps, perpetually apologising for the panic he raised.

'Thump' the door from the street would go, and then we would hear the quick light steps of the younger partner, Mr Gerard, who would take the stairs two at a time, dance neatly around the door of the outer office, grab his post, peer keenly at each one of us from under thick black brows, checking that we were all in place. He would shout 'Good morning,' tilt his homburg if he was wearing it and stride, heels thumping firmly, down the corridor to the extended premises at the back. Most days he wore no overcoat and carried an umbrella only when the rain lashed down. He appeared to thumb his nose at the elements, his quick movements seemingly calculated to carry him between the raindrops.

I liked Mr Gerard and learned a lot from him when he poached me from my regular duties to take dictation. He had a disconcerting habit of pacing the floor while he talked, stopping in his stride to stare over his shoulder at me, and delivering his dictation in short sharp bursts. If he set out to intimidate me he didn't succeed. I would halt him in mid-flight to have unusual legal words spelt out for me, and he was generous enough to pause as he waited for me to write the word in the margin. When we were finished he would throw himself back in his chair and grin companionably, but the companionable grin was absent if the letter was not up to standard when typed; he brooked no shilly-shallying from clients or staff. As I wasn't his secretary I felt he had no interest in me whatever, until one day I had an irate client on the telephone, demanding to speak to my boss and insisting that she had been given wrong information in a letter which bore my initials. Her voice crackled over the wire at such a pitch that I held the phone away from me.

'Madam,' I said when I could get a word in edgeways, 'I gave you the correct information. Mr Gerard is not available at the moment. Please take the matter up with him when he is here. I'll tell him you called.' My hands trembled as I replaced the receiver and I looked straight up and into the eyes of the junior partner as he stood checking the appointments book. Five minutes later his extension buzzed and he asked for me. I took pencil and notebook and pre-pared for a short, sharp burst of letters.

'You did well on the telephone,' he said. 'Who was it?' I told him. 'Nasty woman,' he said. 'You did right to stand up for yourself. In this business, if you feel you're right, always stick to your guns. Well done.'

Shortly afterwards I was reminded once more that he certainly kept an eye on me. When I made my way through town I continued the habit which I had cultivated when I was in school of reading as I walked along. In fact I had it perfected to a fine art. One day as I walked up Fleet Street the book was slapped shut in my face and I stepped back in surprise.

'Are you looking for an early grave?' Mr Gerard growled at me, grasping the book. 'The streets are for walking, not reading. I'll take charge of this.' I felt like a little girl being chastised and I was furious, but there was nothing I could do about it. Last week I had been a competent secretary, today I was a silly child. He kept the book for a week and passed it over without any comment, but I made sure I was well out of the city centre before I did my reading act again.

After the correspondence had been dealt with in the morning, the real work of a conveyancing firm got under way: the buying and selling of property. This entailed a great deal of researching old documents, requests to law searchers for various searches to be carried out in the Registry of Deeds and the Land Registry, and Dublin Castle when a company was involved. I liked nothing better than to clear my desk in the afternoon and set about checking the title to a transaction. The story of a property and with it the story of a family would unfold as I untied bundles of old documents, some of them browned at the corners and detailing a title which had been held for a term of 999 years. I revelled in tracing and deciphering references to plots of land and loved the old stilted English of very ancient deeds, where titles, tenements, hereditaments and fees passed from the party of the first part to the party of the second part, with the whereas, whereby and wherefore scattered all through the documents.

I would have kept the typewriter off my desk all day if I could, as I traced ancient maps and coloured in boundaries and fences. Mr George began to suspect how much I loved this work and involved me in it more and more, allowing me to draw up schedules of documents and spend my time rooting through the boxes in the filing-room, or sending for me to witness clients' signatures and watch the handing over of deeds.

All documents had to be signed, sealed and delivered and a memorial of important deeds lodged in the Registry of Deeds. The whys and the wherefores of all of this was the responsibility of the solicitor, but as I began to be more involved I was initiated into the mystery of writing a memorial.

'A memorial of a document,' Mr George said as he stood beside my desk, 'is a synopsis of the important and relevant details of a property transaction. It must always be written in clear legible handwriting.' He fussed around as I spread the sheet of parchment before me on the desk, looking at me over the tops of his glasses and inspecting the special pen which was kept for memorial writing. He had already dictated the memorial to me in his office and I wished he would stop clucking over me as I dipped the pen in the ink bottle and began to write. I had been warned that the parchment sheets with the first word, MEMORIAL, already printed in ornate flowing script were expensive. I had prepared it as instructed by his secretary, rubbing it gently with a pencil rubber and then sprinkling it with powdered french chalk so that the pen would have a grip.

'Huh,' he grunted as I ignored him and started into my best penmanship, 'this is a very important document.' He dithered until I had passed the first 'hereinafter', then decided I didn't need any more of his guidance.

'The Lord preserve us from fussy old fools,' someone muttered from the desk in front of me, and I couldn't have agreed more.

We overlooked the side door of Bewley's Café, and every morning the secretaries sent out for almond buns, London buns, cherry buns and the occasional sinful chocolate 'Mary' while we took it in turns to make the tea. For the first week I handed out my hard-earned pennies to swell the bulging bag from Bewley's but I could not afford the luxury of a Bewley's bun each morning and counted the cost at the end of the week. The following Monday I lowered my head and clattered awesome speeds from my typewriter as the time for the morning break arrived.

'What do you want for your tea this morning?'

'Oh, nothing thank you.' I glanced casually up and back down again. Silence. I could feel rather than see the glances which were being exchanged.

'Bit of a headache, have you?' the cheery voice asked again.

'Something like that.' As sixpences and threepenny pieces were rooted out from their leather purses, I disappeared to make the tea, wondering if I would have to fake a migraine or barbed-wire sore throat the following day and the days after that. Why, oh why could

I not just say that I couldn't afford the buns, that they cost me nearly half the allowance my mother made me from my salary? For the next couple of days I took my cup of tea to the bookkeeper's room on the pretext of checking figures in one of her ledgers. Miss Moore understood my predicament fully: she never took part in the cake-buying either.

At the beginning of the next week an almond bun was placed next to my cup of tea without a word being spoken. This was the only way they knew of coping with their embarassment. My teeth ached in their gums.

'My mother doesn't like me to have something to eat before my mid-day meal,' I said in my best grown-up voice. I hated myself for what I was saying. My mind hammered out that this was a childish excuse and I was supposed to be an adult now. The voice thumping in my brain lacerated me for bringing my mother into it – my poor mother, who on the days she had visited my father in hospital walked all the way to Bewley's of Westmoreland Street to buy him fresh buns for his tea because she knew he loved them. Oh lovely sticky buns; oh lovely white lies. On the following day, when Miss Moore brought us our brown pay-packets, I awkwardly asked if I could be included in the Bewley's order for that day, and I continued the practice every Friday after that. I had salvaged my pride and the truth was there for those who would read it.

Besides his extensive legal practice Mr Gerard was also a Fine Gael senator whose political activities brought to our office names I had read about in the newspaper. My father had been a staunch supporter of Fianna Fáil and we were all followers of de Valera, whose speech at the end of the war had each one of our family firmly glued to the wireless set. Most of our friends were inclined to the Fianna Fáil party and this brush with what I considered the opposition was a new experience. However, I liked what I saw of the vibrant set of young men who passed up and down the corridors of my office. I basked in the feeling that something new was going on around me, even if I wasn't always sure what.

Not long after I joined the firm, Babs arrived home with a request from a friend who had become involved with the new Clann na Poblachta party.

'Seán McBride is looking for a secretary,' she told my mother, 'and she wondered if Phil would consider the job.' My mother looked at me and shook her head.

'No,' she said, 'it wouldn't be fair to her. I don't want her changing again.'

'Do I have any say in this?' I said from the parlour door.

'I didn't know you were there,' my mother said, 'or I would have told you.' I liked the sound of being secretary to Seán MacBride. Here was a new political party which was getting lots of controversial coverage in the papers, accused of being 'reds under the bed' and involved in all sorts of radicalism. I knew that my mother had visions of her daughter becoming a communist and reneging on her good Catholic upbringing, but I had felt the excitement at work when important people passed us in the corridors, the sense of being present when things were happening and hearing people in high office being discussed, and I liked it.

'I am interested,' I said quietly. 'One of the girls in class went as a secretary to Fine Gael. It's extremely interesting work and she meets lots of people.'

'No,' my mother said flatly. 'I prefer to know the people you will be working with.'

'You don't know the people I'm working with now,' I pointed out.

'I know it's a highly respected law firm,' she spoke sharply to me. 'You are still under my jurisdiction and the answer Babs can take back to her friend is "no". And that's the end of the matter.' I was stung, but in my heart of hearts I knew my mother was right. This 'flashy' job, as she saw it, might quickly fizzle out and politics was something she thought best left to those who had years of experience behind them. There was too much at stake for me.

I was to have another brush with authority, my employer's this time, and again I was to come out at second best. Patsy, who had been a friend since my days in the College of Commerce and who now worked quite close to me on Burgh Quay, suggesting that we 'do' Lough Derg. We had no particular reason for going; we were too young to be searching for husbands, we weren't looking for full-time jobs, and we weren't mothers praying for vocations for our children. It was just that people talked about it and it seemed a good thing to do. It was regarded as the ultimate penance to walk barefoot on the island's sharp stones and go without food and sleep for two nights and, besides, the trip would bring us to Donegal to which we had vowed to return after we had spent a month at the Irish College in Rannafast. Last but not least, we would get three days off work, and no employer would ever dream of docking part of your salary for such a worthy cause.

'Why do you want to go to Lough Derg?' Mr George stared at me intently.

'I want to do penance,' I said piously.

'Are you thinking of becoming a nun?'

'No, nothing like that,' I assured him hastily. 'It's a very big penance, one of the biggest, and I feel I'd like to do it.'

'I know how big a penance it is,' he remarked judiciously, steepling his fingers under his chin. 'I've been there. I'll think about it and let you know tomorrow.' Patsy had already been granted her time off and was about to book the tickets, but it seemed that my employer was about to call in senior and junior counsel to help him come to a wise and just decision. Counsel did not decide in my favour.

'No,' he said, 'I wouldn't feel justified in giving you the time off. Your health wouldn't stand it.'

'Pardon?' I said, my voice disappearing.

'There,' he said, 'I was right. You have a cold. It would be on my conscience if your health broke down as a result of three days' hardship without food or sleep on Lough Derg.'

I choked at the unfairness of it. I hadn't lost a day through illness in the twelve months I had been with the firm.

'Can I take three days at my own expense?'

'No,' he said, 'that's my final word.'

'Maybe he was thinking of your own good,' my mother said, relieved that somebody had put a spoke in my wheel. She hadn't been too keen on my travelling to Lough Derg either.

'I'm entitled to sick leave,' I fumed. 'He's afraid I won't be at his beck and call if I went sick for a day.'

I was angry at being denied this opportunity when I gave good service to the firm and received little enough reward for it. Solicitors' offices were notoriously bad at paying good salaries to staff, because unions had not yet hit the legal profession. Every increase had to be negotiated on a personal level and was given grudgingly. Simmering at this injustice, I began to feel that perhaps it was time to move on.

8

Moving On

I SAT STARING out the parlour window, glumly pondering what had happened. The evening before, Jennie had told me that she had been accepted as a postulant in a Carmelite convent and would be entering shortly after her eighteenth birthday. I could hardly believe what she was telling me. 'A Carmelite convent!' I said incredulously. 'That means we'll never see you again.'

'You will,' she said, 'after a few years. And you'll be able to come and talk to me when I'm no longer a postulant.'

'Behind a grille,' I said, 'that's not much use. Who can talk to a black shadow?'

'You'll manage,' Jennie answered as she turned in her own gate, 'you'll never be lost for words.'

I looked around as my mother came into the room and said accusingly, 'Did you know about Jennie?' Our families had always been very close. We lived three houses apart and Jennie had paired off with me from the time we first played 'pickie-beds'. We had gone to the same school, made our Holy Communion, collected the messages every afternoon and gone to the College of Commerce together. We were the long and the short of it, me tall and lanky, she small, dark and plump. And now Jennie was about to go out of my life.

'I only know what you told me last night,' my mother said. 'These things are usually kept very quiet. It's a very personal thing, becoming a nun. And remember, she had to be accepted by the convent before she could tell anybody.'

Even so, I should have guessed. We were educated by the nuns; we saw them every day of the week; and all of us had at some stage thought about a religious vocation. And there had been times lately when Jennie couldn't join outings we planned because she had an appointment, details of which she didn't share. We had teased her about a secret boyfriend, but she hadn't responded to that. And then I remembered her awkward silences when we joked about nuns and the Church. I should have known.

My mother knew I was unsettled by Jennie's imminent departure, so she put no obstacles in my way when I told her I had seen an advertisement for a shorthand-typist with an insurance company and that I intended to apply. She had reconciled herself to the fact that I wanted to keep moving on, and the opportunities did seem to be there for me. The fact that I had completed a commercial course with the VEC always helped to sway things in my favour.

'We'll look for a second-hand bike,' she said when I raced home from the interview with the news that my new employers had offered me a whopping increase of five shillings per week: they were an English insurance company, and paid better salaries than their Irish counterparts. Things were looking up. I knew I would be leaving the legal work I loved, but insurance policies had their own legal phraseology and my knowledge there would come in handy, or so the branch manager told me.

My new office was in the Car and General Insurance Company at 27 Nassau Street, beside Hanna's bookshop. That was another bonus: I could ogle the books in the windows, browse through the shelves inside . . . and regretfully bid them goodbye. Though I was earning more money now, books in their shiny new covers were still a luxury I could not afford. Instead I took myself to libraries in Rathmines, Kevin Street and Pearse Street, and spent hours rooting through rows of well-thumbed books, with pages and corners turned back and readers' comments scrawled in the margins.

Once again I had joined a staff which was wholly Protestant, though in my mother's eyes the Car and General didn't have the prestige of the firm of JC Parkes on the Coombe: it had no tradition, she thought. What it did have, though, was laughter, good humour and good will, and I quickly began to feel at home there. It was presided over by a genial branch manager who never tired of telling us that he wanted us to be one big happy family. He enquired about our out-of-office activities with great concern, and treated with indulgence our good-looking junior clerk, who started every day by swinging from the lintel of the door to the public office; an exercise, he told us quite seriously, to stretch his arms and legs.

Ours was a small branch of an English insurance company chain, and we dealt mainly with car insurance, which was beginning to pick up now that petrol rationing had eased. When an inspection from head office was expected, we wheeled our bicycles, which we usually parked under the window by the public counter, through the inner office and down the steps to the basement. We each had our own desk and three of us shared the dictation, the form-filling, the issuing of temporary insurance certificates, while I typed amendments, endorsements, insurance policies and the usual letters of a busy commercial office. A very efficient system was in operation: you listed the files you needed and handed this requisition form to our brawny junior, who did the scrambling and the searching for files in the basement below; that evening he filed your carbon copies, so that everybody's desk was cleared before the day was out.

I was again the odd one out as my new workmates talked in the cosy familiarity of a small church-going community, of spring festivals and harvest festivals and people they knew. I was outside their community and they knew it, but with their cheerful interest in me and my family they drew me into conversation and helped me settle into a new office routine. They respected the two years experience I had behind me; I was no longer the junior secretary who manned the switchboard, bought the biscuits, ran for the stamps and posted the letters.

Now that I worked in the centre of town, I joined the hordes of cyclists who swept through the streets every morning to fill the city's offices. Bus drivers, in their cumbersome double-deckers, shook their fists at us as we cycled three abreast and more. The bicycle was king of the road. Cars were of no consequence: there weren't enough of them around.

Most mornings it was plain sailing, down the Coombe and up Nicholas Street where I joined the throng pedalling furiously from Thomas Street and High Street. There were no traffic policemen to halt our flight until we came to the corner of George's Street, where we screeched to a stop if the long arm of the law loomed ahead. Here a large contingent from south of the Liffey joined the fray, six abreast as they wheeled around and fought their way into our stream coming from the city hall. When a policeman was on traffic duty at this corner we rose to his commands, hoisting our rear-ends onto our saddles, but intimidating him by our sheer numbers as we inched forward, each stream a challenge to the other. We piled in front of the few unfortunate cars, wished pedestrians scurrying across the road impolite good-mornings, checked whatever we had stacked on our back-carriers, and waited for the 'off'. When there was nobody on traffic duty, it was every man and woman for themself as we mingled expertly, our brakes screeching, rattling our bells or honking our rubber hooters until good-naturedly we gave way when the encounter looked like becoming too close.

I remember once looking out on the mass of cyclists as I sat on the top deck of the No. 50 bus on Dame Street. I slitted my eyes half-closed and the phalanx of cyclists as they whirred past was like a swarm of locusts I had seen in a nature film.

To make my way to the Car and General Insurance Company in Nassau Street I turned down past Jury's Hotel, making frantic signals to take the right-hand turn across the path of the Dalkey tram which manouevered awkwardly from Westmoreland Street past Trinity College. Crossing over the tram tracks here could be a nightmare, fraught with danger from the shiny tracks and the wooden setts which became treacherous on wet or frosty mornings. We waited impatiently as the seconds passed, watching the big hands of the clock on the front of the college and thinking of the attendance book which had to be signed by nine.

Cyclists heading for O'Connell Street, as I did later, spread across the width of the road as we negotiated the bottleneck which was the beginning of Westmoreland Street. And there he was waiting for us: 'Fingers', king of the traffic cops. He watched us with an indulgent smile as we rounded the corner in a rush of traffic, and when we were nearly upon him he held up a lordly, leisurely hand and we ground to a halt.

Like a general preparing for battle he strode before us taking long, loping strides; Fingers was in control and commanded our every move. His tall spare figure leaned this way and that and pounced when an enthusiastic cyclist, sensing it was our turn to go, broke ranks. It was woe betide him as Fingers hauled him to the centre of the road and lectured him in full view of all and sundry, and kept him there for as long as he deemed necessary as a lesson to the rest of us. Alternatively he would banish the errant cyclist to the edge of the roadway to await a decision as to when he might quietly creep away. When at last Fingers was sure he had us all exactly where he wanted us, he raised his hand, then bending from the waist he swept us past him, his long white gloves dangling from his fist, like some giant fingers waving us on.

In the evening time he loped past *The Irish Times* office to the edge of O'Connell Bridge, twisting his head back and forth to see where the greatest challenge to his traffic-controlling skills lay, daring any motorist to run him down, and we met him again on our homeward run, as Fingers stood at the very heart of Dublin's traffic.

Within a week of starting in my new job my workmates knew that I was a Girl Guide. Two of them were officers in the Blues, and they marvelled at the responsibility I shared with my company captain. They knew little of our organisation, but I was very much aware of theirs – they were the people who had full use of the Powerscourt Estate beyond Enniskerry and could hike and camp within its walls, while we paid for the privilege of having a day's outing there. They had the full resources of a wealthy organisation behind them while we were still relatively new and novices in the game of scouting and guiding. And doing very nicely, I told myself, except for the fact that I would never understand how they were allowed use tents for their camps, and we weren't. Our 'camping' was done under the roof of Marlfield House in County Wexford, a large house which the organisation leased for the summer months.

We continually compared notes, my two Blues captains and I. They were much more relaxed than our association about uniforms and external trappings, and I was beginning to feel the same. Too much time and attention could be paid to shiny brasses, ruled notebooks, stiffly whipped ropes and box-pleats in a uniform. Did it really matter, I thought as I listened to the shouts and screams of youngsters under my control, if some of them turned up in white runners, coloured socks and unpolished brasses? Their mothers were proud of them, loved the fact that they had been accepted into a Girl Guide company and placed immense trust in me as their captain.

I listened to their voices as we sat on the rough wooden floor of the parish hall during a camp-fire, coaxing and teasing individual performances from shrinking violets and discovering a great many aspiring Deanna Durbans and Judy Garlands. When we formed a circle to sing the 'Anthem of Youth', I read out a circular from head-quarters which said that the organisation was thinking of forming a musical society to perform light opera and put on an annual show. This would be a semi-professional performance with a paid producer, a competent student orchestra, a music director and lots more professional help. Opera was a new word to most of these youngsters, but if it meant singing then they all wanted to be in on the act. They had rollicked their way through most of the well-worn campfire songs, and picking up tunes by ear was something they were good at.

It soon became apparent that I would have the whole company auditioning for the chorus, and I was met with long faces when I indicated that the younger ones were not being invited. To the older ones I explained what opera was about and the story behind Gilbert and Sullivan's *Gondoliers*.

'Will the Scouts be taking the men's parts?'

'No, this will be an all-girls' cast.'

'Oh, you mean we have to dress up as boys?' I sensed there might be a falling-off of enthusiasm if their brothers in the Scouts were to be left out.

'You will be dressed in special clothes, like a fancy-dress,' I explained. At least they knew what fancy-dress and wigs looked like.

'Will our mothers have to make them?'

'No, your mothers will have to do nothing. The costumes will be hired from Ging's.' That cheered the doubters up. Ging's was a popular theatre costumier in Dame Street and they all knew where it was.

'All those interested meet me at 2.30 outside HQ on Saturday.'

'They'll get cold feet,' Patsy predicted, 'they haven't a clue about any sort of theatre or opera.'

'Neither had we,' I retorted, 'until we went to the gods in the Gaiety.'

They turned up en masse. Some of them had walked, more had come by bus and a few had borrowed bikes, and they were sitting on the steps outside HQ when I rounded the corner. I worried about those eager little faces at the auditions but I needn't have bothered; we landed the prime roles of Nanki-Poo and Pitti-Sing, one of the three little maids, and the rest of them were selected for the chorus. Puffed with pride, my young troupe didn't miss a single practice thereafter, and the Blues in my office cheered all the way. They offered endless encouragement, sang us snippets of Gilbert and Sullivan, and arrived in a body for the opening night.

The performance was a wonderful success, a sell-out for all three nights. The colour, the fantasy, the wigs, the behind-the-scenes battles with lipstick and make-up, the lights dimming and the audiences' applause, all made up for the long hard weeks of rehearsals. On the final night families gathered with bouquets of flowers and boxes of chocolates which were arranged at the front of the stage for the final curtain.

Later, as the lights in the Archbishop Byrne Hall went dark and the costumes and wigs were flattened into cardboard boxes, I sat amongst sheaves of long-overdue librettos and scores which must be returned to city and far-flung libraries, and felt that a seed had been sown in my youngsters' hearts.

It certainly had. Fired with enthusiasm, the older Guides in the company were ready for any dramatic opportunity which presented itself.

'Can we enter for the Rally?'

'No!' was my first reaction. After all the weeks of rehearsal I needed a rest. I needed to feel that there was a life outside the Girl Guides.

The Rally was an annual concert performance. We had entered a campfire item on a couple of occasions, but had never been successful: every company north and south of the Liffey could do a campfire. But there was an extra incentive this year in that the Gaiety Theatre had been booked for the Rally, and my bunch of budding stars, having tasted the magic of treading the boards, wanted more.

'It can't be a campfire idea,' I began to backtrack. 'It has to be something different. It's just before the pantomine season, so it would have to be a Christmas theme.' I let them think it out for themselves, hoping they'd forget about it.

'We've come up with the idea of a singing Christmas tree,' Mary, one of the senior patrol leaders, announced at our next meeting. It sounded daft enough to be a good idea and anyway I hadn't the heart to say no. So we dreamt up a tableau based on a popular new Christmas song called 'Scarlet Ribbons', which told the story of a young child who wanted scarlet ribbons for her hair and of her mother's desperation because 'all the stores were closed and shuttered, all the streets were dark and bare'. But on Christmas morning a miracle of scarlet ribbons appeared from the tree. The tableau we worked out involved a bed, a child, some angels, a narrator and, most of all, a singing Christmas tree.

Once the idea was accepted we were away. Some girls would hide in the 'singing tree', holding coloured torches to resemble fairy lights; we had scarlet ribbons and costumes for the two angels; the theatre had the bed and the steps for the performers to stand on. As the day of the performance drew nearer there was just one big snag: we had no Christmas tree, and no prospect of one. Christmas trees were not part and parcel of every home.

I was growing desperate but my friend Clare, who lived near a private wooded estate in Blanchardstown, came to the rescue: she knew somebody who knew somebody who worked on the estate and would arrange to get me a tree. But the tree was slow in coming, and when I failed to produce one on the day of the dress rehearsal there was consternation. I assured everybody that a tree would make its appearance for the performance on Sunday afternoon.

'We need another miracle,' I muttered to myself as I rang Clare once again. She hadn't actually got the tree but it would be ready for me on Saturday morning – if I called for it. I sought the assistance of Nancy, one of my senior Guides. We took the bus to Blanchardstown and with Clare's assistance we dragged the tree to the local bus-stop.

'I've no room for that thing on my bus,' the conductor looked at Nancy and me and the eight-foot Christmas tree, his arms crossed belligerently over the straps of his ticket-machine.

'It's for a special occasion,' I tried to explain as heads craned around in the bus.

'I don't care if it's for the King of England himself,' he said, 'you're not comin' on my bus,' and he turned to bang the bell to set the bus in motion.

'We're due on the stage of the Gaiety in two hours,' I begged. The little white lie was easy on the tongue.

'Janey Mac, mister,' came from the front of the bus, 'they must be part of the Panto.' I let that go uncorrected.

'What're you lot doin' with that thing for the Panto?' the bus conductor said.

'It's for Jimmy O'Dea to play Jack and the Beanstalk,' an impatient voice shouted from the top deck. 'Can't ye let the girls on the bus, they're not doin' any harm. It's your good deed for the day, man.' The impatient passenger clattered down the stairs.

'Here, girls, give it a whoosh,' he called and the tree was lifted from our hands and stacked on the open platform, its topmost branch trailing up the stairs. Nancy and I stationed ourselves on each side and held on to the rail as the bus rumbled away towards Dublin.

The tree wasn't heavy, but it was tall and ungainly, and up Grafton Street we wedged it between us, looking neither to right nor left as we pushed along. Past the astonished gaze of the porter on the door of the Gaiety we marched and pounded our Christmas tree into the bucket of sand which was waiting for it. It wasn't the best of shapes but we spent the next half-hour breaking off branches to fill gaps which might reveal the source of our magic voices.

Next afternoon, in a fit of nerves brought on by the size and grandeur of the Gaiety Theatre, our two angels whinged that their cardboard wings wouldn't stay straight and the gold tinsel was falling off; my narrator and principal singer began to lose her voice; the tiny figure for whom the scarlet ribbons were so important began to lose her nerve, and the singers were struck dumb at the thought of the hundreds of people sitting in the audience. It was time for me to do my 'stay cool, act promptly' bit. I assured the two angels that a man in an aeroplane would never see what was wrong with their wings, told my principal singer to find her voice immediately, and threatened dire consequences on anybody who let the good name of the company down. It worked. I watched as the tiny lights of the torches began to wink from the darkened stage, and my little singer trembled and faltered until her pure voice recovered and spun around the theatre like a silver thread, while the stalwarts behind the tree rallied and hummed the backing which gave my narrator support. As they settled into the performance I began to relax, sitting on a step to one side of the stage, and I could feel my arms slowly beginning to ache.

9

Taking Flight

THE BIG ADVERTISEMENT in the paper looked so attractive. Aer Lingus, our national airline, had spread its wings and formed a subsidiary called Aer Línte to operate a new transatlantic service, and they were looking for staff. New horizons were opening for everybody connected with the airline, as they would for all of us in the bright new years ahead, with no threat of war hanging over us. I wanted to be part of that excitement.

My mother didn't quite see it that way. 'Itchy feet again,' she said as she read the advertisement I placed before her. She had given up knitting stockings and jumper suits for us long since, and now concentrated her creative energies on turning skeins of silk into beautiful flowing day-dresses which she threaded with satin ribbon, lining the skirts with taffeta. She had made them for Nance when she was a baby and was now experimenting with an adult one for Madge. 'Itchy feet,' she repeated, clicking the needles and looking at me over her glasses.

'Not really,' I said. 'I like the job I'm in but it gets boring at times, and I'll be at the bottom for ages yet. I can't see any of the staff moving on.' Except for Hetty and George. Well, really only Hetty, because we had watched the budding romance between the two of them and we were all fairly certain that it would end in marriage.

'Yes, but you do get a bonus,' my mother said, 'and in this day and age that is something worth considering. You won't get that in every job.'

I pointed out that conditions were good in the advertisement for secretarial staff, and there were perks attached. I had visions of being offered a job at Collinstown or at the new airport at Rineanna, though how I would get to north County Dublin or further afield to Limerick was something I would have to tackle if the time came.

'Apply for it,' my mother said in the fond hope that I'd never hear from the airline, but I did. The manager in the Car & General was far from happy when I handed in my notice.

'The place is not on its feet yet,' he said, 'and nobody knows if this new venture will succeed. I think you're a very silly young lady and we're all sorry to see you go. If you change your mind in the next month your job will be waiting for you.'

There was no changing my mind: the glamour of working for the new airline and visions of trips to London, maybe even on the new transatlantic flights, outweighed all the cautionary advice I was given.

Because of my legal experience I was appointed as second shorthand-typist to the assistant secretary and legal adviser and I was based in the secretary's office in Upper O'Connell Street. There was no glamour, not even a uniform in sight when I started, except for the peaked cap of the chauffeur who took the higher executive to high places, presumably Dublin Airport where all the action was taking place.

It was made perfectly clear to me from day one that the nature of the work was confidential: we were dealing with reports, consultations at high level and important correspondence. I knew I was witnessing exciting days both for the airline and the country, and I myself was learning some new office routines. Guiding was all around me still. I had left two Blues captains behind me and now found myself sharing an office with one of our district captains and another Guide officer who were senior to me not only in the Guides but in the hierarchy of the office. However, we agreed that because some of our social life was likely to interact outside office hours, we would ban all mention of Guiding while we were at work. Kay, my immediate senior, introduced me to the Gestetner.

'It won't bite you,' she said as she stood beside me at the type-writer. 'The stencils have to be treated gently but they're more resilient than they look,' and she threaded a stencil through the carriage of my typewriter. The stencil was a foolscap-sized sheet of silky wax backed by a page of carbon paper, which protected the wax, and a second sheet of foolscap.

'Leave the carriage loose,' Kay instructed, her hand on the carriage release, 'and switch your ribbon off. The letters bite through the wax, so it's always a good idea to clean the keys before you start.' I gingerly set my margins and my fingers hovered over the keys.

'Don't be afraid of it,' she said, 'it's not the end of the world when you make a mistake. Here's your salvation, anyway,' and she plonked a bottle of correcting fluid beside me. The liquid wax in the bottle looked exactly like pink nail-varnish, and when you brushed it over a typing error and re-typed, hey presto, the pristine wax sheet showed the world how accurate a typist you really were. The 'rolling-off' as we called it took place in another room where the stencil was slotted onto little keys on the Gestetner printer and the stencil carefully caressed over an ink-filled roller. The ink flowed through the type indented on the wax stencil and thus onto the paper, and winding the handle of the printer we rolled off a paper-trail of agendas and reports.

I was in the heart of the city now, just up from Nelson's Pillar whose long column pointed high above our heads. All Dublin life flowed around it: flower-sellers peddling giant chrysanthemum blooms carefully wrapped in huge cones; long queues for the tram to Sandymount and a day away from the hustle of the city; young people standing round its base in the evening, anxiously waiting for their partners. The city hummed between Nelson's Pillar and the GPO, the focus of all nationalism. Opposite my office the Sacred Heart statue had a place of honour, tended by the jarveys who tethered the reins of their cabs to the railings around the shrine, and the statue of Parnell stood majestically guarding the top of the street. Rows of bicycles were parked on an island in the centre, and in the evening 'minders' plied a profitable trade with customers of the Savoy and Carlton cinemas. The Gresham Hotel gleamed with polished brasses and moustached doormen and personified the grace and dignity of this end of O'Connell Street, its once elegant townhouses now turned into commercial offices, and the living nature of the city gathered in caretakers' families high above the streets.

In summer the wide spacious street with its elaborate monument to the great Liberator, Daniel O'Connell, was dusty, sultry and gay with coloured dresses, children twirling paper parasols, and trotting noddies. In winter the glittering lights of the Metropole ballroom and the Capitol theatre and cinema lit the area around Nelson's Pillar like a gentle fairground. The cowlings which had thrown the light of the streetlamps into yellow pools on the pavement during the war years, were removed; lights blazed in shop windows and displays slowly began making their re-appearance after the days of rationing. No window was shuttered; even the smallest shop proclaimed that the long dark days were over and Dublin could reclaim its gaiety.

Determined to see some action in my new job, I made enquiries about the 'perks' which had enticed me, and discovered that the only free trip on offer was not to America but to Rineanna airport near Limerick. Patsy was envious when I told her of my application for a free flight. 'I've never even been on a boat,' she said.

'Neither have I,' I assured her, 'but I'm getting on an aeroplane if it's the last thing I do.'

'Maybe it will be,' she said ominously.

'Aer Lingus planes don't crash,' I said, puffed up with proprietorial pride after six months in the airline. My mother was inclined to share Patsy's view and vowed that she would never fly, as did Madge, my sister. I couldn't ask any of my friends: I could only bring a close relative with me. My enthusiasm and my brave declaration that I was going anyway persuaded a couple of waverers in the office to apply with me, and when Babs rallied to my side, three of us, with three sisters in tow, availed of the limited number of places allotted to staff. We shared a sneaking feeling that there was safety in numbers, and if the plane did crash, which I assured everyone was out of the question, then we would all sink or swim together.

I was sick with excitement as we got on the bus to the airport. Hundreds of people visited Collinstown on Sundays for a day's outing, to stand on the balconies and watch the planes as they zoomed in, but this would be my first time there. My only physical contact with an aeroplane had been when I took a group of my senior Guides to climb Djouce Mountain where a party of French

Girl Guides had crashed. I consoled myself with the thought that that plane had been a small private plane and, despite the trauma of the crash, all of them had lived to tell the tale, which we heard all about when we visited them in St Bricin's Military Hospital.

I had great faith in the DC3 *St Declan* which was to be our carrier to Shannon; nevertheless, we stowed bottles of holy water, miraculous medals and rosary beads in our handbags and checked that our scapulors were safely around our necks before we boarded. As we waited for the announcement of our flight, I silently thanked Aer Lingus for dedicating each of its planes to a saint.

Three of us were Aer Lingus staff and felt we had to dress formally, almost as if we were representing the company. Hats were the order of the day. Mine was of black felt with an upturned brim four inches wide, and as we followed our hostess across the tarmac it spun off in the breeze, bouncing and rolling and pursued by Babs and me in our best high-heeled shoes, to the great amusement of the man fueling our plane. I jammed the muddy hat back on and, dignity restored, approached the steps to the shining silver craft. The airhostess stood on the top step in her neat dark-green uniform with jaunty pill-box hat, calmly took my carrier case, and beamed us to our seats.

I nearly panicked as the door to the outer world clanged shut, our only means of escape cut off. I reminded myself that we were pioneers of a new age and as the plane began to roll down the runway I screwed up courage to glance out the window. My confidence plummeted when I saw just one lonely man at the window of the control tower. We were in his hands, I thought, and closed my eyes tightly as the ground below us began to disappear. When I peeped out again I found myself looking at É I R E printed in glaring white on the roof of the main hangar. I pointed it out to my companions and told them knowledgeably that it was there because of our neutrality during the war, so that any alien aircraft who mistakenly flew over our territory would know immediately who we were.

'Pockets of air,' I explained expansively to Babs as the plane lurched in the sky. 'We're probably going over the mountains.' I averted my eyes from the tiny window; if we were going over the mountains, I didn't want to see.

'Look!' Babs squealed. A whole street of houses and shops was standing on its side below us, and seemed to be getting closer and closer. 'Oh my God, I am heartily sorry,' I gabbled, feeling for my rosary and launching into an Act of Contrition.

'We have just passed the town of Trim,' the pilot's voice boomed over the intercom, 'the aircraft has now turned and we are on course for Limerick.'

'You're a cowardy-custard,' one of the girls behind whispered in my ear. I didn't mind being a cowardy-custard so long as I was alive, and as we rose into the banks of cloud I fidgeted nervously, sneaking cautious glances to see if the wings were still in place. 'A little knowledge is a dangerous thing,' my father had always said, and that was exactly what was happening to me. After six months with the airline I knew of all the things that could go wrong, and in my imagination they were about to. I got no pleasure from flying down over the Shannon and seeing it flowing far beneath us like a ribbon of water. And of course I knew the particular dangers of landing and take-off. As we approached Rineanna I begged Saint Declan to use whatever skills he had to bring this awkward, snub-nosed, ugly great lump of metal safely onto the green grass of his native land, all the while thinking that if Saint Declan in his hermit's cell in Waterford had known anything about aeroplanes he would most likely have condemned them. But somebody heard my cry for help as the plane swung low, dipped and levelled, bounced once off the landing strip, bounced again, steadied, and noisily made its arrival.

'We hope you enjoyed your flight,' announced the voice over the intercom, 'look forward to seeing you on the return journey. Enjoy your day.'

We flattened our hats on our heads, buttoned our coats, gathered our handbags and climbed, none too steadily, down the steps.

'I need two alka-seltzers,' I mumbled to Babs, 'my head is spinning.'

'You had two before we started,' she said, 'no use poisoning yourself. You'll settle down in a while.' I did when the ground stopped imitating the sea and my ears began to recover from their numbness. In the tiny waiting-room looking out at the scattering of makeshift airport buildings, we poured out milky tea from our flasks, the six of us sitting in a prim little line watching for the airport bus which would take us to Limerick city.

We were looking forward to our day. The war years had curtailed travelling, and none of us had been this far south before. I tried to push the thought of the return journey to the back of my mind, though every so often I found myself watching the sky and wondering about bad weather. By the time we arrived back in Rineanna the cobbly-wobbles were under control. I watched our aircraft being checked under and over, the fuel being loaded, the air hostess nonchalantly chatting to the rest of the crew, and thought if they weren't worried, why should I be? I felt immensely proud as I looked out and realised that I was here at the beginning of something new. The people who flocked to Collinstown each Sunday to see the planes taking off would give their eye-teeth to do what I had done today. On the return journey we were all calmer and quieter, though ready with our rosaries and prayers as the *St Declan* slowly approached the airport, circled over the neat semi-circle of buildings, and unerringly touched down.

My mother dreaded the muggy days of November when fog could virtually close the city down. The headlines in the evening papers were never any great consolation to her as we read about cars slipping over unprotected quay walls and other disasters.

'Leave your bike in the office,' she would plead, 'and take a bus home.'

'If the fog is bad enough for me to leave my bike, then you can be sure there won't be a bus running.' My bicycle had become a part of me by now and I wasn't going to leave it behind because of a foggy night. Any cyclist worth her salt was able to brave worse conditions.

Along the River Liffey, just down from our office, was one of the worst places in the city when dense fog enveloped the streets, and as the day continued in a shroud of grey fog we were told to leave early. I carried my bicycle through the door of the office and on to the muffled street. Shapes loomed out of the greyness and I finally took my courage in both hands and crossed to the Gresham Hotel whose lights I could see glowing muddily on the other side of the street. Hugging the channel of the road, I switched on my front lamp, but it was no more than a cigarette glow in the swirling mist. A crowd had gathered near Nelson's Pillar in the hope of getting a tram home, abandoning all semblance of the orderly queuing which had been one of the benefits of queuing for rations during the Emergency. With my eyes firmly on the ground in front of me I pushed forward until I heard the insistent clanging of a tram-bell and a ghost-like tram passed just a few inches from my caped figure. Shocked, I dismounted and began to push my bicycle on the long uphill road home. I had news for my mother.

Within a few months of my free trip to Rineanna the bubble for the new Aer Línte had burst, and those of us brought in to help launch the great new transatlantic adventure faced redundancy. The signs were there for some time; my mother had read them herself in her evening newspaper.

'Where to, now?' she said when I told her, no doubt thinking of the job I had, in her estimation, carelessly slung away.

'I don't know; nobody is saying anything.' We were told next day. The rumours which had been circulating were true: the new Inter-Party Government had decided to scrap plans for the proposed transatlantic route and those of us who had been recruited were being let go. I was beginning to think that I should have taken the job with Seán McBride – he was the one who seemed to be in the driving seat at the moment.

'I got my redundancy notice today,' I said when I came in the door.

'Oh God,' my mother said, 'this means you're out of a job.'

'I'm not out of a job!' I couldn't restrain myself any longer. 'I've been offered a job in a new firm of solicitors.'

'You've what?' My mother could hardly keep up with me.

'One of the partners is a sister of my boss in Aer Lingus and he has recommended me to them. They've agreed to take me on his recommendation. And I've got a bonus from Aer Lingus as well. I'll get a bonus of £28 when I've worked my notice – eight weeks' salary!'

My relief at having a job to go to was tempered by the fact that there would be no more free air-trips, no more concessions to distant destinations. I would be firmly back on solid ground, returning to the seriousness of a solicitor's office. Air travel would have to float out the window for a very long time to come.

10

New Horizons

MISS FEENEY HAD been a sergeant major in the British forces during the war and she fully intended to retain her status as she set about managing the firm of solicitors of which I was the newest member. She began her instruction where I was concerned by initiating me in the mysteries of the dictating machine. She frog-marched me into the inner sanctum used by the two partners in the firm and pointed to a small microphone which they used to record dictation. The message was transmitted onto a wax cylinder by a needle which bit into the wax, and a further machine sat on my desk ready to receive the scored cylinder. 'This,' she said, 'is the receiving end; put those things in your ear and listen.' I heard the voice of my new boss gabbling rapid instructions.

'It's too fast, I can't understand a word he's saying!' Miss Feeney plucked up the tiny buttons suspended on a band which clipped across my head, nearly taking the tops off my ears so that I yelped.

'Sorry,' she said, 'let me listen,' and she slid into the typist's chair which I had quickly vacated. The wax cylinder, she instructed me, must always be handled with the utmost care and carried with two fingers of each hand inserted at either end; no sweaty fingers must touch the surface. A third machine sat on a window-table beside my desk; this shaved a fine film of wax from the used cylinders and left them clean and ready for further use. The wax cylinder sat in containers of six and were treated with immense care: a careless knock against a desk and a whole morning's dictation would lie in smithereens on the office floor.

Miss Feeney never spoke of her experiences during the war; it was almost as if that part of her life was over and she intended to get on with the next, starting with this young and vibrant team of which I now felt proud to be a part. She was in charge and she made no secret of this. She rarely barked at me, but crossed swords on many occasions with the powers-that-be, two young solicitors in their early thirties who had put their years of apprenticeship and employment with a reputable firm behind them and decided to branch out in partnership. Their exchanges often climaxed with a sudden eruption from the inner office, and Miss Feeney would march out, her chin jutting out and her shoulders squared above her military-trim, slim-clad hips. For the next half-hour she would bang the keys of the typewriter in short angry bursts and answer the intercom in a very clipped tone. I left her to it: the mood would soon pass off and she would be her cheery self again. She was good to work with; she made it perfectly plain that she was the senior secretary but we shared the work equally. Each morning she scanned the *Legal Diary* and moved quietly and efficiently to have files and forms, documents and details in readiness for any court appearances that day. She arrived in the office on the dot of nine, left for her appointed lunch-time no matter who or what threatened, and her scheduled bus in the evening allowed her no time for dallying after office hours. Organised and punctual in everything she did, she simply had no time for anything that bordered on the inefficient.

Unfortunately this was a young firm trying to find its feet in a profession peopled by old and well-established companies, and every day was a challenge. The firm intended to handle all types of work; nothing hopefully was too big and nothing was ever too small. Four of us shared two offices overlooking College Green: our lady solicitor, who also supervised the firm's finances; her partner, our ambitious driving force, and Miss Feeney and myself. We availed of the services of a part-time Costs Drawer, who was a mine of information and experience which we drew on time and time again, and we also had a part-time Summons Server. Short-staffed at times and forever watching court dates and legal deadlines, I learned the routines of District, Circuit, High and Supreme Courts and parts of the city centre I had never heard of became real living places, where tiny solicitor's offices hid away at the end of dark hallways or perched four storeys up at the top of worn stairs. Because I had a bicycle and was willing to be out and about, I learned to serve Notices of Appearances, Notices of Motion, and signed and sworn Affidavits on uninterested clerks who skulked behind their empty outer offices until I banged the bell loudly for attention.

The exciting thing about my job was one never knew what might happen from one day to the next. The pressure of work kept us on our toes and its variety kept our brains ticking over. Everybody pitched in when the going got tough, and we sat on the edges of one another's desks comparing documents which had flown through the typewriter to make sure that every 'i' was dotted and every 't' crossed. The work I was doing brought an intensity to every day and the following-through of a case was immensely satisfying. I was in a welter of legal bamboozlement and loving every minute of it.

I began to look forward to seeing a row of cylinders stacked on my desk in the morning. One of the solicitors would have worked late the night before and it was my job to prepare his brief for counsel. With the file and the revelant reports gathered neatly in a basket, I was away. My solicitor had a clear analytical mind which unfolded the story of the plaintiff and the defendant and set out the precedents he had culled from the many legal books ranged on the shelves in his office. He would quote medical reports, engineers' reports and actuarial reports and give his assessment of damages, all of which would be laid before one junior counsel if it was a Circuit Court case or two for the High Court. They, having done the donkey work, would pass their comments to their senior, who would already have received his own pristine copy of the brief from me. It was my job to type the story and make sure that counsel had each and every one of the revelant reports. The brief-paper was then folded in four, properly dated, headed and signed on the front portion, filled with the incidental papers and tied with pink tape. Either solicitor would then trot down to court to find the counsel of their choice. That was always a matter of personal contact.

'Have you a hat?' My boss looked at me hopefully from the door of the inner office. I had lots of hats, if he really wanted to know.

'Yes,' I said, puzzled by the question.

'Have you got one here?' he said patiently. 'I need somebody to go to court urgently, and I'm tied up.' As it happened, I had taken a beret with me that morning as I intended going to confession in Whitefriars' Street on the way home.

'Take your bike,' he said 'and get to the Four Courts as quickly as possible. You'll find junior counsel in Court No. 2. He's just rung to say he'll take this brief,' handing me the packet I had just assembled.

'Why the hat?' I looked to Miss Feeney for enlightenment.

'You won't be allowed inside the court without a head covering. And what's more,' she said 'you weren't engaged to run messages. If he wants a messenger, let him get one.'

'Oh, maybe you're right,' I muttered to myself as I hawked my bike from the back of the downstairs hall, but I forgot all about Miss Feeney's disapproval as I cycled like mad up the quays and turned over the bridge into Chancery Street to catch junior counsel before the courts closed at four o'clock. Whatever Miss Feeney thought about the rights and wrongs of whether I was a secretary or a messenger, I really didn't care; swinging the pink beret in my hand I negotiated my way along the corridors until I located Court No. 2.

'Can't go in there, Miss, without something on your head.' My way was barred by a uniformed usher. I fixed the beret on my forehead and the usher pushed open the door. A case was in progress; absolute silence prevailed except for the rustling of papers and a lone voice talking in legal jargon. I stood rooted to the floor, intimidated by the solemnity of the court. One or two heads turned and glanced at me. The man I sought was sitting in the front bench; I had difficulty recognising him with the pompous wig which nearly obscured his features. The usher, noticing my hesitation, whispered, 'I'll take that for you, Miss. Where is it to go?' I clutched my brief tighter. It was my responsibility to deliver it to my junior counsel: those were my instructions. In my imagination I could see myself in the dock and a barrister asking severely, 'Did the witness deliver the parcel into the hands of the man for whom it was intended?'

'No thank you,' I breathed. I tiptoed forward in fear and embarrassment and stood at the side of the bench. Junior counsel sensed rather than saw me. We spoke in whispers. I looked at the judge who was almost within reach, and expected him to say at any moment,

'Six months for contempt of court,' but he just glanced over his glasses and resumed his reading. I wasn't sure what was going on in Court No. 2, but nobody was as tense about it as me; everybody looked relaxed and even bored. I had a feeling that the sight of me in my summer dress and pink beret was a welcome diversion.

I welcomed trips to Dublin Castle to research companies or to the Registry of Deeds if a date on the title to a legal transaction needed checking. If I didn't do it, one of the solicitors, whose work was more important than mine, would have to. Miss Feeney considered these matters outside her secretarial skills and duties, and besides it would have taken her all day whereas I was prepared to walk or cycle wherever I had to go. Overtime she also declined, so it was left to me to spend the extra time in the evening if a case suddenly demanded attention.

'There's a man at the door to talk to you,' Betty called, arriving in a flutter into the kitchen. It was Saturday morning and the house as usual was being turned inside out. My boss stood just inside the hall-door.

'I need some important documents typed this weekend,' he said. 'Can you come in this afternoon?' I agreed straight away, but then he hesitated. 'It's a rather unusual case,' he stumbled, and I had never seen him so embarrassed. 'I'm not sure that your mother would approve of you working on it. Perhaps you should ask her.'

'My mother is not here at the moment,' I said, wondering what criminal were we about to defend.

'It's a matrimonial case,' he said, 'an application for an annulment. Your mother might not like you typing the details.'

'I'm likely to come across that sort of thing at any time,' I said breezily, not having a clue what kind of details such a case might reveal. I was more concerned about the fact that he thought the typing might spill over into Sunday: *that* was something I would have to sort out with my mother.

'Miss Feeney wouldn't give up her weekend to work on this important case,' I told her when she came in, 'so he's more or less depending on me.'

'What's the hurry?' she wanted to know.

'It's something to do with an application date for something or other which has to be in by Monday,' I said vaguely. I had never come across an annulment beyond knowing that it was something the Catholic Church granted to dissolve a marriage in very exceptional circumstances. I wasn't about to burden my mother with it. The fact that I had worked on Sunday must be mentioned in confession, but in the mean time I classed it as necessary servile work, and let the sad details of an unfortunate marriage flow through my fingers.

As a child I had often envied the people who could watch from windows during a parade. Now I had a first-class vantage point as our office was on the route of the parade to the GPO on Easter Monday 1949. I waved when a child raised a tiny tricolour on the street below.

At one minute past midnight that morning I had stood silently with my mother and sisters at our open front door, wrapped against the chill of an April dawning. We listened as a twenty-one gun salute blasted from O'Connell's Bridge to commemorate the men of 1916 who had raised the flag of Irish freedom thirty-three years before. History was being made and we were part of it. Bonfires were blazing on the Dublin hills.

Military units from Collins and Griffith barracks paraded at the head of the march, with the Army No. 1 Band and the Garda Band followed by armoured cars which drew sustained applause from the crowd. The men and women of the voluntary auxiliary forces, the ARP and the LDF, wore camouflage tin hats and reminded us again of black-out curtains and their hammering on people's doors to extinguish lights during the Emergency. We cheered the infantry in their brightly polished, nearly-red boots, the bicycle brigade, the Red Cross and the sailors of the Slua Muirí with their wide swinging pants and jaunty hats, while overhead a squadron of Spitfires of the Irish Airforce flew low over the city.

When the parade had passed, we turned on the wireless which somebody had brought to the office. History was about to be made. The radio crackled as we tuned in to Radio Éireann to hear the declaration of the new republic:

'The part of Ireland heretofore known as Éire ceased as from the eighteenth day of April 1949 to be part of His Majesty's dominions.'

As the crowd erupted in cheering I looked down on historic College Green and thought of Grattan, and the Irish Volunteers, and all the many attempts to assert the rights of Ireland. Now we were no longer the little country of Éire who had held valiantly to its neutrality when forces stronger than ours threatened our shores. We were Ireland, a strong voice among the nations of the world.

We stopped at a newsagents just below the office, Patsy and I, to buy sweets for our journey home.

'I wrote to the King,' the little figure with the top hat and cane was saying to the man behind the counter. 'I wrote to the King,' he repeated with bristling belligerence, 'and told him I wanted to remain a British citizen and loyal to the crown.'

'And did ye get all dressed up to tell him that?' the shopkeeper said, eyeing the striped waistcoat and the gold chain, and the red rose in the lapel.

'My good man,' the loyal fellow said, pocketing his ounce of tobacco, 'I dressed up to see the parade!'

That evening a group of us pedalled up the wide Chesterfield Avenue of the Phoenix Park, to mingle with the crowds who had assembled to watch the fireworks display laid on by the Army Command. While searchlights, redundant since the ending of the war, danced intricate patterns against a velvet sky, we danced impromptu variations of the Walls of Limerick and the Hokey-Cokey and gathered en masse to sing 'Auld Lang's Syne.'

We younger people, citizens of the new republic, were discovering reasons of our own for dancing and dressing up. When Christian Dior, the great French couturier, and his talented pupil Yves St Laurent launched the New Look, the clothes-coupons of the war years were brushed into oblivion and the new post-war fashion swept through the streets of the capital. The New Look was demanding: it insisted that we all follow the trend, and a generation which had grown up with hand-me-downs and turned garments was suddenly falling over itself to adapt to the new flowing styles. The New Look lowered the length of skirts and coats by at least six inches, more if one preferred, and the tight military style of squared shoulders and narrow skirts blossomed into graciously swinging coats, skirts and dresses. Suddenly clothes which had been in fashion one week were out of fashion the next. The New Look simply took over.

To switch our old clothes to the new style, we took perfectly good winter coats which still had lots of wear in them, had five or six inches of contrasting material inserted above the hem, or extended the hem by the addition of a large band of astrakan or fur. Trimmings shops set up in every street to cope with the demand for braid to cover tatty hem-marks or fraying edges as we stretched our hems to their limits. *Haute couture* was the 'in' word. Dressmakers sprang up like mushrooms and their names and addresses became closely guarded secrets. The drab greens, greys and blacks of the war years were discarded as new materials – none resembling khaki – found their way into the big drapery stores, where it became imperative to devote a whole department to materials for dressmaking. It seemed that all at once there were huge varieties of cloths; rivers of silks, satins and linen flowed tantalisingly beside the old reliable tweed and *báinín*. Nylon made an appearance, in various strengths and startling colours; it had been developed during the war for parachutes and military coverings and its toughness was legendary.

'Nylon stockings in Clery's of O'Connell Street.'

'How much?'

'Half-a-crown a pair.'

Expensive but worth every penny: they were indestructible. Then manufacturers got wise, modified the tough thread, and nylon stockings really took off.

Every aspect of fashion benefited from the New Look; even the shoe manufacturers took up the challenge and two-tone tan-and-white shoes became the rage for summer wear. Other colours followed – black, white and navy, or green and blue – and for those who didn't want to spend precious money on keeping up with the changing scene, Woolworths sold a paint guaranteed not to crack with wear, which of course it did. The amateur could also try her hand at hat-making to complement her plunging hemline and new shoes. White scrim hat shapes could be bought off the peg and covered with fake fur from the renovated winter-coat or draped with bunches of silk or nylon flowers to match summer's long flowing or full-skirted dresses.

Haute couture needed a lot of money, especially when the price tags displayed on the wax models began creeping steadily upwards. With my new-found wealth courtesy of Aer Lingus's redundancy payment, I was eager to be out there experimenting with the New Look.

'It's burning a hole in your pocket,' my mother said, 'but then it was an unexpected windfall so enjoy it. But mind,' she raised her finger, 'you put some away for a rainy day.'

The sun shone the day Patsy and I set out to buy our New Look coats. She was an only girl and the pride of her father's eye, and both of us were in the money. The fitted beige coat I tried on reached well below the calf of my leg and was the height of New Look fashion, the assistant assured me, as she carefully pinched the waistline while I preened myself in the mirror. Patsy's was a soft apple green which complemented her wavy auburn hair. We bought hats to match – 'in for a penny, in for a pound' we decided – and mine, brown to match the buttons on the beige coat, hugged my head and swept out in an arched brim which dangled a self-spotted veil to the tip of my nose.

'You'll never walk in those!' Hoots of laughter greeted me when I arrived home and displayed the new shoes I had bought in Saxone of Grafton Street. They had felt comfortable when I walked along the floor of the carpeted shop, but I was beginning to have my doubts now as I walked up and down in the kitchen.

'The very latest in shoe fashions,' the assistant had insisted, 'they're called wedgies.' From the front they looked like very high Court shoes, but a wedge of light wood, triangular in shape and covered in the brown suede of the shoe, was set into the space normally allowed between sole and heel. They were three inches high.

Our new finery needed to find an outlet and where better than the Dublin Horse Show. We tottered there on unsteady feet and sweltered in the autumn heat until common-sense finally told us to divest ourselves of our long sweeping coats, discard the ridiculous shoes, and we relaxed in the sunshine. The coats cut a dash at Sunday Mass and we paraded them to a meeting of Guide officers to a chorus of 'oh's' and 'aah's', and though my mother shook her head at my extravagance, I think she was secretly pleased. The dreariness of wartime was gone, hopefully for ever. Hems crept back up again eventually, but the New Look had been a challenge when it was most needed and held out new promise for the future.

Working as I now did close to Dublin's fashionable quarter, I had ample opportunity to explore the shops at lunchtime. I would often slip around the corner to Suffolk Street to gaze at the beautiful fountain-pens set out in an enticing display of marbled colours in the window of The Pen Corner, or step into Walpoles, drapers to the gentry, where one was 'madamed' by a uniformed flunkey and 'madamed' again by beautifully-groomed assistants in black day-dresses, who, under the eagle eye of a supervisor in striped trousers and black tails, literally pounced on customers in their efforts to effect a sale. Walpole's spelled class and its clientèle was very wealthy.

Trams clanged around the corner of Trinity College as I turned up Grafton Street. There was a special warmth about Grafton Street, a feeling of opulence and restrained wealth, which emanated from the plush interiors of Switzers and Brown Thomas, and was perpetuated by the doormen dressed in braided overcoats who ushered privileged customers to their waiting cars. Then there was the glitter of gold and silver from the window of Weirs the jewellers and the quiet decorum of its showrooms; the fashionable shirts and suits displayed in Kelly's the Gentlemen's Outfitters, and the ornate doors of the Sweepstake Office.

Grafton Street and Nassau Street were rich in smells: the scent of perfumes mingled with the rich aroma of Havana cigars, so that the musky sour smell of cheese in Lipton's was like a welcome return to nature. At the top end of the street the pungent smell of roasting coffee-beans combined with the sweet aroma of pastries from the Monument Creamery, whose almond rings my mother loved, and above it all came the cosy, comforting smell of cooking from Jammet's famous restaurant on Nassau Street, haunt of the rich and famous, with its exclusive menus and dinner-jacketed waiters.

The upper half of Grafton Street was plebian by contrast. Nobletts sweet and tobacconist shop set out to tempt the Gaiety's pantomime crowds and filled its windows with every imaginable confection, from the delicious Hedji Bey Turkish delight to the lowliest form of Jelly Baby. Here the great Woolworths emporium drew crowds of shoppers through its swinging glass doors. This was Dublin's superstore. It sold everything, playing havoc with household budgets as array after array of toys dazzled childish eyes, though it was not only the children who were seduced; there were many things there for the adults too, from inexpensive jewellery to every kitchen utensil ever conceived. It was hard to resist the beaming smile of the talented young lady sitting at a piano beside the sheet-music stand, who would rattle off your favourite piece if you asked her. Another sale made.

I loved Grafton Street, with the embrasured windows of its former townhouses set high above the street. I often tried to visualise its past as I strolled by.

'Nice houses, lovely places in their day.' A voice behind me jolted me out of my dreaming.

'I seen ye standin' there lookin'.' He stood outside McConnell's fish shop, wearing a striped apron which matched the striped canopy over the shop-front.

'I was wondering who used live there,' I said.

'Wolfe Tone did, right over there in No. 69,' and he pointed at the windows over the Singer Sewing-machine shop.

'He eloped, ye know,' the fishmonger informed me. 'Brainy fella Wolfe Tone. Should'a stuck to his law books.'

Grafton Street was Dublin at its best, colourful, tantalising and gay with its shop-awnings and uniformed functionaries who felt they owned the street and all who shopped there. Dirty as it often was with belching buses, litter and discarded fruit and flowers, it still retained a sense of style and elegance with its wealthy shoppers in fox-fur and fur coats. So many shops on Grafton Street evoked an old fashioned feeling, like Vards the furriers, Wines antique shop, and Combridges where messages from the shop floor to the offices above were relayed through a horn-shaped speaking tube. It reminded me of Frawley's of Thomas Street where I spent many hours as a child while my mother did the shopping, and I spent my time watching the passage of the money-containers which sped across the ceiling from the counters to the counting-house above the shop. Grafton Street was like that too, warm with people who never seemed to hurry and had time to stand and talk and tip their hats and nod graciously to the world as it passed by.

11

Are There Roads in Rome?

'I'M GOING TO Rome.'

'Yes?' My mother bent over the tapestry, busily tracing the stitches she had missed as her needle wound wool in and out through the canvas she was working. She had discovered tapestry and for the moment all knitting and crotchet was suspended in favour of the new craft. A tapestry of 'The Angelus' was already framed and hanging on the parlour wall.

'I'm going to Rome,' I announced again.

'Hardly by aeroplane,' she said, 'you've left that behind you. You must be walking or cycling?'

'I mean it, Mam,' I said, absentmindedly flinging my Guide books on the chair where I had been told umpteen times not to leave them.

'I've just washed that chair-cover,' my mother pointed out. 'Take your books upstairs or they'll go into the pound.' The pound was a system agreed by us all to keep an active family of girls from cluttering up the living-room with books, scarves, hats, handbags or anything else that might be discarded in the rush of the moment. The fine we paid to get them back went to 'Madge's missions' – money she was collecting for an order of missioners in Africa. The system worked on and off, and although nobody took it too seriously, it concentrated our minds when we were reminded.

'The Pope has declared 1950 as a Holy Year, and we're making a Holy Year pilgrimage.'

'Who are "we"?'

'I've just been to a meeting in the Guide headquarters. The organisation is planning to have fifty people go to Rome for Easter of next year.'

'That's a whole year away,' she said, thankful that she had time to adjust to the notion.

'It gives me only just enough time to save for it,' I pointed out.

'How much?'

'Fifty pounds.'

She looked at me. 'That's a lot of money,' she said, 'you'll never save that amount.'

'If I save a pound a week, I'll do it,' I said. Fifty pounds to save in fifty weeks for 1950 – the figures rounded up nicely.

'Go ahead then,' she said, 'but I'm warning you, you have a hard time ahead of you.'

On Christmas Eve of 1949 Pope Pius XII would knock in solemn ceremony on the holy door of St Peter's Basilica in Rome, and this ceremonial opening would be the start of *Anno Santo*, the traditional Holy Year celebrated by the Catholic Church every twenty-five years. The Holy Door would remain open until the following December, and during that time pilgrims from all over the world would flock to St Peter's Square to gain the special plenary indulgence known as the Jubilee Indulgence. The month before the opening of the Holy Door would be a special time for me. On my twenty-first birthday I would officially come of age, could vote in a general election for the first time and be able to say, if any argument arose,

'I'm 21 now, so I can do as I please.'

Not that that statement would hold much weight with my mother.

My friend, Patsy, who was also running a Girl Guide company now, and I were the only two of our group who had signed up for the pilgrimage to Rome. Everybody else decided it was too expensive, and they didn't relish the hair-shirt regime we proposed for the next twelve months. I was now responsible for my own clothes, so my weekly allowance, adjusted to take care of that, would be more than ample to allow me save the fifty pounds I needed as long as there were no more new clothes, no scone and cake teas in the Monument Creameries, and no trips to the theatre. Patsy and I had the same allowance, thirty shillings a week.

The adventure would be worth every penny we saved and every time I turned from the blouses and dresses in the shop windows, I reminded myself that the excitement of travelling abroad, of seeing

London and Paris and the long length of Italy, would more than compensate.

'If there wasn't a Holy Year do you think we'd have thought of travelling abroad?' Patsy asked one day as we leaned on the handlebars of our bikes and thought of the long summer months ahead with no holiday to plan.

'We wouldn't,' I said decisively, 'none of us would have dreamed of doing anything like that on our own. Think of all the planning and finding places to stay.'

'You're right,' Patsy agreed, 'but I wish it wasn't such a long time away.'

Through the long months of summer we found it hard to maintain interest and more than once felt like giving up. The memory of the previous year's holiday was still fresh in our minds. Five of us girls had left Dublin on a Saturday morning with no more definite plan in mind than that we were heading maybe to Killarney. We had joined *An Óige*, and we had a map and a list of *An Óige* hostels. None of us had any experience of hostelling, and it soon became apparent that we were novices at the game compared with the hostellers from England, with their shorts, their up-to-date equipment and bicycles with dropped handlebars and intricate gears. Nothing daunted, we had pressed on, pushed our bicycles to Mountain Lodge Hostel and breasted the rising roads of Mount Melleray, where there was no room at the inn. As a result, we all spent a sleepless night on the floors of a very damp B&B, and not having the heart to complain to the newly-married couple who had opened their doors for us, we beamed delightedly at them next morning.

After seeing the splendours of Killarney, we entrusted our five selves and five sturdy bicycles to a wizened old man who ferried us across Lough Leane.

'It's bottomless,' he said sucking in his cheeks and rolling his eyes when he had taken us to the murky centre of the lake. 'Aye, bottomless, they say. If ye fell in there now, girl, it's out the other side of the world you'd come for sure. They might find us all in Australia.'

We made it to Kenmare and drove the warden's dog mad by dropping pellets of paper down on it through the gaps in the dormitory floor, and we sat up in the hostel in West Cork for half the night, shoes at the ready to chase black beetles back to their holes in the wainscotting. We cycled from Roche's Point, oblivious and uncaring when the clouds opened, and could hardly have got wetter if we had gone swimming on Trabolgan beach, but we changed in the toilets of the railway station in Cork city, put our heavy bicycles in the guard's van and travelled in style back to Dublin. We had had a wonderful fortnight for that holiday, but spartan times were now upon us as we kicked our heels and waited for Easter 1950. We boosted our morale by patting ourselves consolingly on the backs and saying that having put our hand to the plough there must be no turning back.

My worst moment came when three-quarters way through the year, Thomas Cook and Son sent out a short note to tell us that due to circumstances beyond their control, etc, etc, the fare would be increased by ten pounds. Oh well, I thought, I could now give up the struggle without losing face.

'I just can't afford it,' I told my mother.

'Yes, you can,' my mother said. 'I'll help you out. I'm proud of what you're doing,' she said, reading the notice from Thomas Cook. 'I'll give you the difference and you can hold on to your whole salary for the four weeks before you go. You'll need it for pocket-money.'

I was silent. I knew how hard things had sometimes been at home, and here I was imposing another burden by my determination to go on this pilgrimage and my need to prove to her, and indeed to myself, that having started something I was prepared to see it through.

'It's okay,' my mother said quietly. 'It's not been easy, but things are a lot better than they were and you've all helped.'

My twenty-first birthday came just before Christmas. My friends and sisters' friends gathered into our house and brought me presents geared for my trip to Rome. Nobody we knew had ever travelled this far before, and the presents reflected our idea of how to prepare for a long journey. I ended up with enough toilet bags, talcum powder, bars of perfumed soap and hankies to supply the whole pilgrimage. Nightwear, a dressing-gown, underwear and stockings, all beautifully presented, littered my bedroom and peeped out of the case which now sat ready and waiting for my departure some four months away.

My mother arrived home from the January sales, bulging with pride and a coat-length of wine-coloured woollen cloth she had bought.

'You talked about making yourself a coat,' she beamed. 'The girl in the shop put everything together for me. What do you think?' I jumped for joy. My New Look coat was hardly the thing to travel in through Europe. I knew exactly what I wanted: a swagger coat, loose and comfortable, snug and warm to keep out the cold winds we were likely to encounter in early April. Making my own clothes gave me great pleasure, and Babs, who in her spare time had taken a dress-designing course, helped me with patterns for dresses and skirts. Making a coat was still a big challenge, even though I had looked for the simplest style in the Vogue pattern book.

My mother sat tensely in her chair as I spread the woollen material on the parlour floor and knelt to pin the pattern in place. My mother's cousin, Willie, who lived close to us since they had sold the farm in Wicklow, rat-tatted at the door; since my father's death he had kept a big-brotherly eye on us and never passed the house without checking to make sure that we were all in one piece.

'Rome wasn't built in a day, Peg,' he counselled my nervous mother as he looked at the jigsaw of pieces floating under the legs of chairs and watched me adjusting lengths and widths. 'Let her away with it. What harm if she makes a mess of it? It won't be the end of the world.'

I looked gratefully at him and tried not to show the frustration I was feeling as the intricacies of the pattern unfolded. The finished coat wouldn't have won prizes in a tailoring competition, but my mother took it to a professional button-holer, and then bought a yard of velvet and helped me fashion a plush collar to set off the coat.

Already Holy Year crosses were being erected on hills and mountains around Ireland, and it was as if people were suddenly waking up to the possibility of travel beyond England. A new eagerness and restlessness was replacing the tightness and caution which had followed the years of the Second World War. Betty, now working on the clerical staff of CIE, joined the pilgrimage at the last minute. As an employee of the railway she enjoyed a concessionary fare, and my mother came up trumps once more with a loan of the balance which Betty paid off on her return.

We were the first pilgrimage to leave Dublin in that Jubilee Year. Well-meaning friends and families arrived at Westland Row station armed with Qwells, Alka-seltzers, Aspros, headache powders and barley-sugar sweets. The excitement which had been building up for weeks, of obtaining my first passport and changing carefully hoarded pocket-money into travellers' cheques and foreign currency was over, and I was beginning to experience my first feelings of panic. For one wavering moment I wanted to turn the clock back and forget about all this fuss. The feeling passed as we boarded the boat-train for Dun Laoghaire. Photographers' bulbs flashed as we were solemnly blessed, and the morning papers carried the news that fifty Girl Guides were embarking on one of the biggest adventures of their lives. It was Sunday, 2 April 1950, and our well-wishers went home to their snug beds while we braved the depths of the Irish Sea on the *Princess Maud*, with a long night's journey ahead of us.

My first voyage was not the sweetest baptism. We huddled on deck while the ship lurched towards Holyhead on a rough sea. Patsy was uncomfortably sick and lay wan and quiet for the whole crossing, and I wished myself back home half a dozen times before the boat docked. Patsy and I had opted to forego our officer status in the matter of dress so that we might have the honour and glory of carrying our company colours in whatever parading there was to be done, but I moaned in complaint as I carried not only my own company flag, but Patsy's as well, along a cold British Rail platform at one o'clock in the morning. She was too green to care. I slung a leatherette bag containing two long poles, a heavy poplin flag and a leather holster on each shoulder and struggled along like a trussed chicken.

The train steamed into Euston Station at 6.30 in the morning and a little later, breakfastless and without a night's sleep, I didn't want to see the beauty of Westminster Cathedral as we took our places for an early Mass. Then we were off again for Newhaven and the crossing to Dieppe.

Dieppe was the real start of 'abroad', and we listened eagerly to the hum of French at the quayside, the chatter of workers in their navy berets as they hauled on anchor–chains and mooring ropes and drew us alongside the quay wall. My legs felt like jelly as I steadied myself on French soil; two sea-journeys behind us, and we gathered our belongings and boarded the train for Paris, sleep now the all-important thing.

Paris in April. Nothing very different about the railway station except that it was larger and much busier than Westland Row. We held grimly to our bags as zealous French porters tried to grab them from us, and answered them in English and Irish until they raised their hands in despair and decided to leave us alone. A bus took us to our hotel, the Terminus Nord, where we gratefully washed ourselves and our underwear and stockings, and a long leisurely rest on a real bed had even the sickest among us sitting expectantly in the dining-room for our first taste of foreign food. There were mutterings of disappointment when perfectly normal soup was served and no snails appeared despite the dire predictions of those we had left at home, but the lovely white French rolls disappeared by the basketful. Bread didn't taste like this in Dublin. Since the introduction of bread rationing, we still hadn't quite got back to the fluffy white bread of my childhood.

Our spirits were bubbling again as we piled into taxis for a tour of Paris by night. The guide-books we had pored over for weeks came alive as we swung from window to window to see the Arc de Triomphe, the Eiffel Tower, the Rue du Bac, the Bastille, the Opera House, the Seine. Time was too short for even one little walk along the Champs-Élysées, but what mattered most was that after months of waiting we were in Paris, and we would go home and tell those at home that we had been there.

'Tea,' I said to Patsy, 'I need a cup of tea.' No tea or coffee had been served with the evening meal, but the café next door stood invitingly open.

'Tea in a glass!' Eileen said in disbelief.

The waiter beamed at us as he placed a glass with a labelled muslin bag before each place.

'Where's the tea?' Tea at home meant big fat juicy tea-leaves skulking at the bottom of the pot.

'It's in the bag.' We fished around with our spoons.

'Where's the milk?' Cubes of brown and white sugar sat in dishes on the table, but there was no milk. 'Anybody know the French for milk?'

'When in France, do as the French do,' I said, remembering the dictates of the tourist guide, and nearly had the maligned tea poured over me.

'*S'il vous plaît?*' The waiter hovered with a dish of thin lemon slices in his hand.

'*Merci,*' I beamed, and he slid a lemon slice into my glass, added a cube of sugar and bowed. I stirred, sipped and discovered I was sold on tea Continental style.

We returned to the hotel to queue for much needed baths and to inspect the weird arrangement of washing facilities in the bedroom. We contemplated for a long time the extra item beside the wash-hand basin, set low on the bedroom floor.

'It's a toilet,' Patsy said.

'The toilets are on the landing.'

'For washing underwear?' she hazarded.

Not sure of its function and unwilling to display our ignorance by asking, we decided it was a footbath, and for safety's sake left it severely alone.

Another five a.m. start and the train rattled through vine-covered hillsides in an unending vista of olive greens and arid patches. The landscape looked bleak and cold. This fourteen hour journey would be the longest of the pilgrimage and we slept propped against each other, gathered in groups in the corridors, sang, prayed and consulted our guide-books as the train wound its way towards the Italian border.

'I don't think I could look a hen straight in the face,' I complained to Patsy as I took yet another hard-boiled egg from my lunch-box. Patsy was past caring. We walked her up and down, fed her Alka-seltzer and Fox's glacier mints and I planned to buy a bottle of cognac and dose her with it when the train stopped for a customs check at Modane.

It was a weary, disgruntled troop which arrived at the Hotel Milano in Turin. Although relishing the extra hours in bed the following morning, I was none too pleased when the powers-that-be decided that, as this was a pilgrimage, we should make an effort to visit the Salesian College of St John Bosco to pray at the shrine of Dominic Savio, the boy whom the Pope was honouring with canonisation later in the year. Our special pilgrimage tickets allowed for *no* deviation from the planned timetable, so my hopes of taking a stroll around the streets of Turin went by the board.

Back on the train again, the last leg of our journey to Rome would take the best part of ten hours. A contingent of Catholic Girl Guides from Holland had joined the train. They were dressed in the international blue of the world-wide organisation and were fascinated by our distinctive brown. They were astonished at how far we had travelled and curious about Ireland, a country they associated with England, and were surprised to learn of our separate identity. Carefree and carrying little luggage for their two-day journey, they teased us about our two uniforms, one for travelling, the other kept specially for our audience with the Pope. We sang and exchanged campfire songs, swapped badges and addresses, and vowed to meet again.

Further south the train ran along the coast, and the Mediterranean glinted in the background. We had passed Genoa, and as Piza swung by in the distance we craned to catch a glimpse of the famous leaning tower. Towns on the Italian Riviera with romantic names like Rapallo and Capri, places we had read about and until now had never dreamed of seeing, were tantalisingly close as the train shrieked and dashed over the rails. It was midnight when we arrived in Rome, one thousand five hundred miles from home.

The weariness of the long overland journey was soon forgotten. Rome would be ours for a week. Our first day was Holy Thursday, and the Catholic Church was celebrating. We went to early morning mass in the Church of St Mary of the Angels, where we mingled with hundreds of Romans all bent on honouring the great Feast of the Eucharist. The sun which had abandoned us for most of the outward journey shone as we set out to visit each of the city's four basilicas. A Jubilee visit to the basilicas, with statutory prayers recited, were the main conditions of gaining the special Holy Year indulgence granted by the Holy Father.

We entered St Peter's Square in the tradition of the medieval pilgrimage, the national flag and the flag of the organisation at the head of eight standard-bearers as we climbed the cobbled incline to the steps of St Peter's, reciting prayers as we came. The Irish poplin flags emblazoned with gold and embroidered emblems fluttered in the morning breeze and with my leather holster low on my hip to steady my swaying pole, I was very proud, there in Rome, to carry my company's standard. Our entrance caused quite a stir and had *Osservatore Romano*'s roving photographer scuttling around us to get a picture, copies of which were flashed home to Dublin and printed with the headline: 'Dublin Girl Guides Arrive in Rome'.

'*Anglaise*?' An Italian lady poked me in the shoulder, ignoring the fact that I was saying the Jubilee prayers.

'*Irlandese*,' I said and pointed to the badge on my shoulder and the national flag.

'Ah . . .' she said and I knew that she didn't know from Adam where Ireland was.

It was infuriating to me, then and in the days that followed, to be confused with English tourists. We were very Irish and wanted everybody to know it: exactly a year earlier we had heard our land declared a republic in its own right.

'I'll carry a map with me,' I said fiercely one day.

'What's the use?' Eileen said in her gentle way. 'We'll only be a dot on your map as far as they're concerned. And it doesn't matter anyway.' But it did to me. We had travelled a long way to be in the Holy City, and I wanted people to know where we had come from. The Italians weren't remotely interested, however. Their Pope, and he was very firmly *their* Pope, had invited the whole world to St Peter's Square in this Holy Year, and so they gave everyone the loudest welcome possible. They clapped and cheered as we held our heads high, braced our shoulders, fluttered our flags and approached the Holy Door which had been ceremoniously tapped with a silver hammer at the commencement of *Anno Santo* 1950.

'I can't take it all in,' I said as I stood inside the door of the great basilica which was filled with the murmuring of groups reciting prayers.

'Don't let your flag touch the mosaic on the floor,' was hissed at me. 'Mosaic' was a new word to all of us, but would become very familiar in the days ahead. Under the vigilant eyes of officious ushers, we folded our flags and returned them to their cases.

'We'll never see everything,' I said in despair as we were hurried forward to look at the high altar and the canopied chair of Saint

Peter. We lined up to kiss the toe of the great bronze statue of Saint Peter, and studied Michelangelo's marble *Pieta.*

'Let's get the Jubilee visits out of the way before we do the sightseeing,' our chaplain advised. 'Rome,' he said, 'needs more than one visit, and most of you will return sometime.' We assembled again in the afternoon and marched to the Basilica of St Mary Major and then to St John Lateran, the parish church of the whole world. That was three of the obligatory visits finished, and the fourth, to St Paul-outside-the-Walls, must wait till the following day. As the Irish College was close to St John Lateran we called in to see it. We inspected every room in the place and particularly the room where Daniel O'Connell, the great Liberator and orator had died.

Rome was bathed in early summer sunshine on Good Friday as we made our way outside the walls of the ancient city to St Paul's, on the great Appian Way. After a while I wandered away from the others to be alone with my thoughts.

I kicked the sandy path and scuffed my feet in the gravel much as I had done as a child when I wanted to think seriously about something.

'*Quo vadis, Domini?*' Peter had said to Christ, who looked at him sadly and barred his way somewhere here on the Via Appia.

'I go to take your place,' Christ answered him and the terrified Peter, fleeing Rome and the certainty of prison, pain and execution, looked long and hard at the Man who had told him that he was the rock upon which His church would be built. I thought for a long time about Peter's road back to Rome along this dusty Appian Way, his fear and apprehension, courage and determination.

Later that day we joined the crowds who silently pressed forward to kiss the crucifix laid on the altar steps of St Mary Major, and took our place in the long queue to climb the steps of the *Scala Sancta* or Holy Stairs. These, we were told, were the original stairs up which Christ walked on the first Good Friday when he was taken before Pilate, and which St Helen was reputed to have brought from Jerusalem. The sacred footprints were protected, and we climbed the stairs on our knees.

Afterwards we came down the hill through a cobbled street lined with stalls, where Italian housewives prodded at heads of cauliflowers and squeezed the fruits to test their ripeness. Our eyes drifted longingly towards slices of blood-red melon, so tempting in the mid-afternoon heat. Cheese, smelling sour and pungent, stood on the counters in blocks, while the Italian women accepted offerings for tasting presented on the end of long glittering knives. Nowhere did I see narrow oblongs wrapped in silver paper which was the cheese I knew.

Below the market and the plaza of pavement cafés stood the giant crumbling monument of the Coliseum. Wandering up and down the cold stone steps to the galleries was chilling, and unforgettable. It didn't need much imagination to visualise the events which had taken place there. Gathering together with the other groups there, we recited the Creed and affirmed our solidarity with the martyrs whose blood had stained the great amphitheatre in the early days of Christianity when Rome and its empire was at the height of its power.

We had been allocated seats for our audience with the Pope in the Tribune of St Veronica, high above the heads of the crowds gathered below in the basilica. The big moment of our pilgrimage had come.

It was the custom to name large pilgrimages in the Pope's welcoming address; our small contingent had hoped for, but hardly expected, a mention. Then we heard, 'To the Girl Guides of Dublin . . .' in the high, thin Italian voice of the pontiff.

'*Dia lenár bPápa*,' rang out three times in response from fifty strong young voices wild with excitement.

'You could hear that shout clearly outside the basilica,' a young Irish priest told us later.

Fifty white handkerchiefs waved at the pontiff as he was carried past us after the audience; he looked across and waved back. The Pope knew we were here! He knew we had travelled all those weary miles to see him!

The papal audience on Easter Saturday brought our official visit to a close. We had fulfilled the conditions of pilgrimage.

On Easter Sunday morning we rose with the Italians. Rome always wakened early. The clatter of trash-cans being emptied and voluble voices calling in the street shattered our sleep at about 5 a.m. each morning. The city was about its business while we were wearily rubbing sleep from our eyes, but then it lowered its blinds for a two-hour siesta in the middle of the day, and people shrugged their shoulders at the tourists who had the madness to stay on their feet. But this was the day when the heart of Rome would be filled to overflowing. This was the day when the exuberant Roman would join the tourist throngs and share their Pope with the whole world.

It was imperative to get to St Peter's early to join the Pope as he celebrated High Mass and broadcast his message, *Urbi et Orbi*, to the world. We were in Rome with him, and our voices would be carried on the crackling airwaves to the brown wireless-set in our little living-room where my mother and sisters would be sitting listening. After early Mass to receive Holy Communion, and a rushed breakfast, we joined the groups gathering at the Bernini columns which surrounded Vatican Square and took our place in the long queues being slowly marshalled into the Basilica of St Peter. The throng of people cheered and waved wildly when the frail, ascetic figure clad in the full regalia of Supreme Prince of the Church was carried past on a ceremonial chair lifted head-high by Swiss Guards, his right hand in a perpetual motion of blessing. Every neck craned forward, every eye looked upwards and cameras flashed and clicked and whirred. For a moment as I looked at the heavily guarded and resplendent figure, exalted over the heads of the crowd, I thought of how lonely he must feel. But the thought passed and I joined in the singing, the shouting and the babbling of many tongues.

Mass over we fought for space at the barriers held in place by the Papal Guards. Hoisting myself half-way up on a barrier, I could see people filling the square and massing as far as I could see down the long avenue of the Via de la Conciliatione. The multitude listened in silence as Pope Pius XII, in the first great Christian gathering since the cessation of the Second World War, spoke of peace and reconciliation. A great, great quiet descended on the vast congregation as the slim figure, divested now of his ceremonial robes, his long, white soutane and white skull-cap standing out against the grey basilica, raised his hands in blessing to Rome and the whole world.

It was impossible to see all that Rome had to offer. We rose most days at impossibly early hours and skipped the siesta, but were still making plans at midnight for the next day's sightseeing. Time was much too short and I felt handicapped by our lack of the language. Fortunately for Patsy, Eileen and me, I had managed to make contact with the Carmelites at Collegio San Alberto. Armed with their telephone number I shouted 'Pronto' into the phone and kept repeating the name 'Brother Michael' until a familiar Dublin accent eventually came on the line.

'Push your way forward from the moment you step on the bus,' Brother Michael said when he came to the hotel to take us on a tour of the seven hills, four of which we walked with him.

'Use your elbows,' he said; 'you can't be ladylike when you travel in Rome.' We were learning to adapt to Rome's transport.

'Watch me,' he said as he forged his way past fat Italian ladies with unwieldy baskets, calling '*Permezzo, permezzo*' firmly.

'*Permezzo*,' we chorused behind him.

'Don't sit down,' he commanded as we dived for an empty seat at the side of the swaying bus. 'Hold on to the bar above your head and keep pushing forward.' As everybody else had the same idea, we were soon glaring at one another, no quarter given. The battle of the buses was on, and it added zest to our days as we lunged and gasped when the driver swung his bus around corners or shot across the path of oncoming traffic, and expected us all to join in the valedictions he heaped on the heads of young men scooting perilously close on tiny mopeds and lambrettas.

'Watch your money,' Brother Michael warned, and we patted our bulging breast pockets and balefully dared any light-fingered entrepreneur to even consider trying.

'If anyone pinches you,' he said in an embarrassed tone, and we opened our eyes in surprise, 'just stamp hard on his foot.' They hadn't told us anything about this in the lead-up to the pilgrimage. When the pinch came, it came from an unlikely quarter. The offender was a tiny, inoffensive-looking, middle-aged man who nipped my bottom as he passed with his briefcase. Although the stamp on his foot wasn't nearly as hard as I had planned, he looked at me in pained surprise, hardly uttering a yelp.

'A good kick in the ankle, he'll hobble for days,' was the brisk advice of a nun in the Marymount Convent where we were taken to sample the one and only good cup of Irish tea of the whole fortnight.

'The Italians,' she said dismissively, 'and indeed the French too, don't know what tea is,' and she poured the lovely warm liquid into china cups and filled us with Irish soda-bread.

'*Quanto costa?*' Brother Michael taught us to say when we went hunting for souvenirs. In the shops we had at first depended on the honesty of the assistants when we displayed our money and invited them to take what was needed, but under his tuition our bargaining skills improved and we no longer accepted the first price mentioned. We made long lists of people who might expect a souvenir from Rome. We examined Holy Year medals of all shapes and sizes, miniature statues, the likes of which had never been seen in Ireland, but the biggest success of all was the 'flicking Pope' which I discovered in a tiny shop on the Via Nationale. It was a series of pictures of the Pope in a small notebook, and when the book was flicked, card-shark style, the benevolent pontiff blessed everything in sight, his right hand flowing with remarkable accuracy down the length of the pictures.

'I don't think they'll let you through customs with that,' Patsy protested when I paid over a hefty wad of lira for a clock set in a metal case resembling the dome of St Peter's.

'Who's going to tell them?' I challenged as I wrapped the precious gift I had bought for my mother at the bottom of my bag and covered it with a wet sponge and towel. Replicas of my precious clock were sneaked back to the hotel in the following days as word got out about my purchase, and dire consequences were threatened on anybody who spilled the beans to the courier or a senior officer.

Following Brother Michael's pointer for a sightseeing short-cut, we climbed step by impossible step up the winding stairway to the Dome of St Peter's, where we were pointed to the Castel d'Angelo, once the fortressed home of the popes, and saw the Tiber snaking past the city. We clicked our cameras to show everybody at home that we had looked into the manicured gardens of the Vatican, and we waited and hoped in vain for a glimpse of the Pope in person. We dragged weary legs along the corridors of the Vatican Gallery and stared at the glories of Michelangelo's art on the ceiling of the Sistine Chapel. The chapel was dark with the gloom of many years, and my main interest was in the row of thrones along one wall. This was where the Pope was elected. These were the thrones in which the cardinals sat while the momentous God-inspired decision was sought. I looked in awe at the canopies over each throne and imagined the awful moment when one was lowered over the man chosen as the successor in the line of popes since the time of Peter. For me the glories of the Sistine Chapel, its paintings and mosaics, paled as I contemplated these seats of power.

On the last day of our touring with Brother Michael we went to Michaela's Catholic repository, a shop much like Burns, Oates and Washbourne at home. Here they specialised in ordering and executing Papal Blessings for young couples about to be married. On the day of the wedding, together with the telegrams of congratulations, the best man would give pride of place to the blessing executed on a roll of parchment and stamped with the seal of the Holy See, and it would then be framed and hung in a prominent place in the new home.

Brother Michael probed us gently as we treated him to lunch before we said our goodbyes.

'Twenty-one,' he mused, 'it's time you decided what you're going to do with the rest of your lives.' We agreed that it probably was.

'I was eighteen when I made my decision,' he went on.

'And my mother was my age when she married,' I said.

'Well,' Brother Michael said, not letting any of us off the hook, 'which is it to be, marriage or the convent?'

Patsy and I looked at each other, and Eileen and Mary, who were with us that day, dropped their eyes in confusion. None of us had a boyfriend in mind, so it looked as if marriage was out of the reckoning for the moment. I looked from the windows of the café where it overlooked the Via de la Conciliatione, watching the little knots of black-robed figures, with so many different wimples and head-dresses, the flowing black skirts of clerical soutanes and the brown and white habits of tonsured priests. They were a special part of God's family, specially chosen by Him; but there were so many of them in Rome that day that I felt it would be impossible for me ever to find out what each of them did as part of that great whole. I knew what a priest did, or that the most important thing he did was the celebration of the Eucharist, but nuns . . . I felt a stirring of resentment which I quickly dismissed that nuns, somehow, did not share what I felt was the better path. I would have had no hesitation in choosing to be a priest, I thought, as I looked at Brother Michael who was due for ordination himself in a few years' time.

'Well?' Brother Michael was waiting for an answer, and he followed my gaze out to the people-filled street below.

'Tell you what,' I said flippantly, 'I'll do one or the other before the end of this Holy Year, I promise,' and I nearly said, 'cross my heart and hope to die' but realised in time that I was now a mature twenty-one-year-old and must act accordingly. 'I'll enter a convent or marry a man.'

The other three gaped at me.

'That's a tall order you've set yourself,' Patsy said soberly. But Brother Michael twinkled conspiratorially and said, 'Atta girl!'

This was too serious a question to be decided, no matter how lightly, on this particular day in Rome, but I had the feeling that having turned twenty-one decisive action was needed to shape the rest of my life. I knew that with this momentous pilgrimage behind me, I would go back and seriously consider where my life was going.

The long journey home began in the early hours of the morning, as all our travelling seemed to do. The city was grey and cold when we waved goodbye, the train taking us on the first leg to Milan, via Florence and Bologna, where we were to attend a gala performance of *Aida* at La Scala. High up in the top tiers of the theatre, our seats gave us a bird's eye view of the stage below, the grand sets and the sumptuous costumes and the glitterati of Milan, garbed in ball-dresses, diamonds and tiaras and waiting solemnly for the performance to begin, opera-glasses poised. We had been warned that opera in Milan's prestigious theatre was a serious night's entertainment, so not a whisper escaped us as the sonorous sounds of Verdi's opera rose and fell. I was expecting applause and lots of it when the audience deemed it was deserved, but I was unprepared for the booing when a performer failed to enchant. We felt sorry for the bosomy sopranos and contraltos and the hefty tenors, basses and baritones, so we cheered and stamped with those around us when they were pleased and refrained from the cat-calls and whistles of derision when a high 'C' slid off the top or the conductor's baton caught a singer off cue.

Our route from Milan was called the Simplon route and took us on a scenic journey past Strésa and the Italian lakes, past the customs post of Domodossala and then on to Lausanne and Lake Geneva with the Swiss Alps providing a backdrop I was never likely to forget. This was my dream. On that train journey I stood rooted to the open window. Rome I would swap any day for some time in the icy grandeur of these mountains. I was Heidi sitting on the uplands, making garlands of eidelweiss and cornflowers blue as the sky, and I conjured up mountain monasteries with St Bernard dogs carrying barrels of cognac to skiers trapped in avalanches.

'Switzerland is where they can cure TB. Fill your lungs with that wonderful air.'

'I don't have TB,' Eileen said indignantly.

'I didn't say you had.' Everybody in Ireland was touchy about TB. It was the forbidden disease, never talked about, never owned up to; even to mention it struck terror. Young people seemed to be its target, and mothers watched in fear for tell-tale signs.

'All I'm saying is that Switzerland has the best TB doctors and sanatoria in the world,' I said and dropped the subject. It was not a bad place at all to be sick, I thought, as the little village of Aix-les-Bains in the French Alps slipped past, leaving my dreams of Switzerland behind.

'You'd make a small fortune if you could bottle that air,' the courier said, 'but close the window like a good girl before we all freeze to death.'

Paris was but a stop on the way home. There was none of the excitement or anticipation of the outward journey. We were jaded travellers, transferring from Victoria to Euston in the cold of a bleak April evening to face once again the night journey from London to Holyhead and on to the Irish boat. The sea was calm and we huddled under our rugs and slept, conscious that the comforts of home awaited us on the following morning.

We all gathered on deck to get our first glimpse of the Irish coast, our flags and bags light on our shoulders as Howth slipped past and Dalkey appeared on the horizon. As we watched the early morning mist swirl along the coastline, a voice in a lovely soft lilting Donegal accent spoke from the rail of the ship:

'Oh Ireland isn't it grand you look

Like a bride in a rich adorning.

With all the pent-up love of my heart,

I bid ye the top of the mornin'.'

I gripped my case and looked to see where Betty was, and swallowing my emotion, I knew that we were safely home.

Two days later, as I cycled up Vauxhall Avenue, a neighbour's child stood with arms outstretched barring my way. I hesitated. This particular child had to be treated gently.

'Yes, Pat,' I said as I skidded to a halt. He gripped my handlebars.

'You've just come back,' he said. I nodded, thinking he might ask for a medal.

'Do they have roads out there?' he said, 'are there any roads in Rome?'

12

Standing at the Crossroads

I HAD SOME currency left over from my Rome trip: the precious English five-pound note which we had had no opportunity of using, some francs and lira, and I thought it might be enough to replace the cardigan of my mother's which I had lost on the journey. However, a cheque for the full amount of the cardigan arrived from Cook's travel insurance, so I still had my foreign currency to play with.

'Ten whole Irish pounds,' I said gleefully to my mother when I arrived home from American Express. 'Ten whole pounds, and I saw a grey topper in Gleeson's of Camden Street; it was £9.19s.'

'And . . .' she said expectantly, watching me as I fidgeted with the ten-pound note.

'I thought it would go with the green . . .'

'Buy it,' she said, 'if you like it. I'm sure you need it.' I needed it. Twelve months of spartan living were behind me. It looked as if there could be life after Rome!

Yet for a while the pilgrimage we had done continued to dominate everything. Rome fever was catching on and suddenly it seemed as if the whole country had decided to go on a Holy Year pilgrimage, now that people could look beyond our shores again. It was as if we had been the first to blaze the trail, and I was constantly questioned about what we had seen and how far we had travelled. I had kept a tiny diary of the daily happenings, words jotted quickly which I could hardly read on my return. A priest friend who had asked me to expand the diary read the finished piece and passed it on to his novices who would in time spend some years studying in Rome. I had no objection to telling people about the journey but suddenly called a halt after a tiring evening spent answering innumerable questions in Irish after I had given a talk to *An Réalt*, the Irish language section of the Legion of Mary.

Other things were happening. The office was moving from College Green to College Street, and it meant weeks of rearranging office furniture. We were also rearranging office staff, for Miss Feeney now decided that it was time for her to move to Kenya, and compared to Kenya my little excursion across Europe paled in significance. Her departure was unsettling, not only for the office because we now had to think of new staff, but I was also beginning to think that maybe there might be life beyond the confines of College Street.

I was now the senior legal secretary, in charge of the two newly recruited junior staff. The work of the firm was expanding and in a short time we were able to employ a full-time law clerk and a book-keeper. We were a big happy family, each helping the other and no one so isolated or specialised that they could not put their shoulder to the wheel during a crisis.

'There's a sale on in Richard Alan's in Grafton Street.' Noreen, our bubbly little redhead from Kerry, was constantly in straitened circumstances when it came to replenishing her wardrobe. 'I saw the dotiest little cardigan suit,' she said eagerly, and we all looked at each other.

'How much?' I said resignedly. We knew what had to be done. We would form a clothing club, each person paying an equal share for the number of weeks corresponding to the number of people in the club. Noreen would be given number 1 and she could go off happily and buy her 'dotiest' little whatever-it-was, and faithfully pay back her 'divvy' to the clothing club each week.

This was a young office. The partners gathered about them young professionals of their own age when work demanded. Our junior counsel were young men already making names for themselves in the legal world, our architect was young and eccentric and highly talented, and the doctors consulted for their opinions were already courting the prospect of senior positions by recommending senior men to us for High Court cases, all of whom were consistently used so that the office had started to build quite a name in the legal world.

The offices were on the fourth floor, and the window beside my desk, looking over the treetops and roofs of Trinity College, gave me an uninterrupted view of anybody walking from the direction of Grafton Street. This stood us all in good stead on the day we decided to cut out a summer dress for Mary on the carpet of our lady solicitor's office. I had just sliced through the glazed cotton in a wide sweep of skirt when the look-out at my window announced that one of the partners had just passed Trinity College gate. I knew exactly how much time I had left, as I snipped and cut and delegated Mary to pick up every thread from the floral carpet. The dress and pattern were nicely wrapped and safely in Mary's bag when we heard the lift gates bang on the fourth floor, by which time we were all innocently tapping away at our typewriters.

Compared with other solicitors I visited in the course of my work, ours was a reasonably modern office. There was no clutter of sagging files on ugly looking shelves and file boxes gathering dust in the corners, although there was plenty of clutter when an emergency presented. Then you walked gingerly over files, papers and bundles of documents, and heaved a sigh of relief when the case for court walked out in the brown leather briefcase of whichever solicitor had caused the rumpus. But in general strict rules were set out and strict rules were obeyed. Diaries of court cases were kept up to date, closing dates of conveyancing transactions were carried forward and the office for the most part ran smoothly. 'Closed' cases were kept in a huge roll-top press which took up the whole wall of the main office. It lent an air of opulence to our rooms when the slatted mahogany front was closed fully, its polished surface gleaming softly in the light. There was a mahogany desk in each solicitor's office, and I would sometimes run my hand over their green leather tops; I loved those offices with the tall bookcases filled with thick leather-bound volumes, their gilt lettering bearing heavy legal names which were reverently quoted in long legal battles.

'Why doesn't he give you an apprenticeship?' Miss Feeney had asked me one day when we had spent hours checking documents and setting out title to a long-tailed estate. I was startled.

'You're young enough,' she said. 'I wouldn't be bothered; I'm not going to stay with the law for the rest of my life, but you could. You're interested, as he well knows.'

'You need lots of money to become a solicitor,' I said to her, and plenty of money to pay Law Society fees, I wanted to add.

'He could waive the apprenticeship fee if he wanted,' she said. Our conversation was purely casual, and Miss Feeney had since left. She had planted a seed which could never really grow. I didn't dare aspire to being a solicitor – it would have been stepping out of line. Though our office had a woman solicitor, women were only beginning to push their way into the professions and were regarded as 'blue stockings' encroaching on male preserves. Girls were expected to marry, and to leave work on marrying. I thought we might have been encouraged more, but the times and my background were against it.

Brother Michael had been right in Rome when he said it was decision time. I hadn't enlightened him then that I had already made one feint at convent life, and wasn't in a hurry to try again. The first attempt could so easily have ended in disaster.

It had happened during my last year in the College of Commerce. From about sixth class in primary school in Weavers' Square we had talks from 'visiting sisters' both from the Mercy Order and from nuns of missionary orders, all intent on inflaming our hearts with a desire for a religious calling. My mother had always listened to our reports of the visitors and never said aye or nay.

'Time is on your side,' she would say, giving no hint of whether or not she was prepared to part with any one of her six daughters. 'The nuns are silly to think that you should shut yourself up in a convent at fourteen years of age. Once in, you can't come out.'

And she was right. If a girl entered a convent she was expected to stay there. In the case of the boys, a 'spoiled priest' was every family's nightmare. Vocations were a way of life in some families, particularly in rural areas. Sisters followed sisters and aunts, and families were proud to have two or three sons in the priesthood, the way set out before them by uncles and grand-uncles. My mother would never have the blessing of a priest in the family, and I would look with envy at pictures in the paper of an elderly couple kneeling to receive the first blessing of a newly ordained son, and think of the pride it engendered, of the sacrifices made and the respect it demanded. It never seemed fair to me that, because we were six girls, our family could never be able to command all that pride and respect.

'Sure ye can rest aisy, now, Jack,' I overheard one joyous morning after a first Mass had been celebrated and people were pumping the hand of the proud father, 'the eldest the priest, another goin' for the doctorin', and the third to bring up the grandchildren. Now, but you're the snug man entirely.'

My disastrous encounter with the religious life happened when I read an advertisement in the *Irish Catholic*. A new Italian order of nuns, situated in London, was seeking English and Irish postulants. Unbeknownst to my mother I wrote to them. Letters to our house were few and far between so that their response, addressed to me with an English stamp, caused quite a stir. I opened it in the privacy of my bedroom, and the stir was nothing to the hullabaloo and the uri-ari which erupted when I announced my intentions.

'You're what?' My mother leaned heavily against the kitchen table and sat down.

'I've applied to join an order of Italian nuns, and they'd like me to come to London immediately.' I shook in my shoes. I hadn't a clue how to get to London to begin with.

'A convent in London?' My mother drew in her breath. 'Let me have a look at that letter.' She read the letter which was in stilted, broken English, though the instructions were clear enough.

'You're not going,' she said as she anchored the letter on the window-sill.

'I am,' I said stubbornly and I rushed out of the room and up to the bedroom. There was silence from the kitchen below; the wireless was switched off while my mother concentrated. I had to admit to myself that it had come as a bit of a shock. The reality of what I contemplated, of going to London and eventually to Italy which I only knew from my atlas, suddenly hit me. I stared out the back bedroom window at the narrow hedge and my mother's wallflowers and suddenly they became the most important things in my life. Even the painted gate at the bottom of the yard filled me with nostalgia. The sounds of my youngest sister Nance and her friends playing skipping on the road below pricked the back of my eyes, and I blinked back the tears.

Dinner was a silent meal. Everybody now knew what was in the letter.

'Whichever of you is down to do the dishes, get on with it,' my mother said as she disappeared up the stairs. At this stage I could have said to my mother that I had changed my mind, but in all our minds was the fact that this was an official letter. My mother felt it had to be dealt with.

'I'll be back in an hour,' my mother announced when she reappeared with her coat and hat on, pulling on her gloves. 'Nobody leave this house until I get back.' She lifted the letter from the kitchen window and folded it into her handbag.

'I've made an appointment for you to see one of the priests in Whitefriars' Street,' she said on her return. I knew she was easier in her mind, and I also knew that there was no way for me to chicken out of the appointment.

'Aren't there enough good Irish convents here if you want to try them out?' the priest said briskly when we met. 'And I've told your mother that. I've also told her, and I'm telling you now, that Irish girls have the reputation of being great workers, and some of these foreign orders are trying to poach our best girls.' Nothing more was said, and the letter went unanswered. I wasn't pleased with myself for what I had done, nor for the worry I had caused my mother.

Jennie had entered the Carmelite convent when she had barely turned eighteen, and Brother Michael in Rome had done the same thing. Several friends who had either been in school with me or in the Girl Guides suddenly announced they were entering convents, and in most cases it wasn't the most holy among us who made the momentous decision. In some cases my friends' mothers were heartbroken as they parted with their daughters, proud that God had chosen them, but sad that some would never again cross the family threshold. There was a bewildering number of orders, with different regulations as to postulancy, noviceship, professions and whether they took a simple vow or a solemn vow. Although the orders varied in their purpose and work, all were united in the one great purpose of service to God for the rest of their lives.

Time was marching on. I liked the idea of considering a vocation and praying about it when I went on weekend retreats with a group of friends, which were becoming very fashionable. The rule from the evening of arrival was silence and contemplation until the last meal on Sunday, when tongues were loosed and all the religious exercises safely tucked away for another year. Retreats were also a way of excusing ourselves from the parish mission and satisfying my mother that I was looking after my immortal soul.

Even though I was pushing myself to make a decision, I knew somehow that the religious life was losing out. It was a good option when the only other path expected of us was marriage and the rearing of a family, but increasingly I wondered if I should concentrate my energies on that goal. So I began to put thoughts of a vocation to the back of my mind, to be taken out and examined occasionally, particularly when we went to visit Jennie. Nothing had made her swerve from the path she had chosen. We rarely saw her face but even the black-veiled grille could not hide her happiness and the warmth of her greeting for us. Her novice mistress, on the other hand, was as interested in our activities outside as she was in Jennie's progress inside.

'What are you wearing today?' Mother Joseph's sprightly voice would ask from the convent side of the parlour. We told her about the New Look, the high-heeled wedgies, the cummerbunds, the tight waspies of thick elastic webbing which circled our waists and flared the skirts of our dresses over our hips. We discussed skirt lengths, jackets, hats, and told her the price of everything. I became increasingly sure that I belonged on my side of the grille.

It began to be a disadvantage, having no brothers in the family. Brothers could be relied on to escort their sisters to parish hall 'hops' on most occasions. Once there they attached themselves to the rows of boys on one side of the hall while their sisters lined the other side with all the other girls. I went a few times with Patsy and her two brothers, and hated every minute of it. We both spent more time in the cloakroom combing our hair and smoothing our dresses than we did on the dance floor. The embarrassment of not knowing if we were the target of any of the shy – or brash – looks from the well-turned out, oil-slicked bunch on the other side of the hall had us on more than one occasion retrieving our coats and heading for our bicycles in the parking lot.

Dances in town were frowned upon unless you had an escort or went in a group, but we still often studied the Friday night *Evening*

Herald and *Evening Mail,* both of which had a full page of advertisements for dances on Saturday nights in various halls throughout
the city centre.

'It's all countrymen's associations,' Patsy pointed out. 'The
Meathmen's Association, the Cavanmen's Association – every county
in Ireland seems to have an association, and they're all running dances.'

'And they'll all be full of countrymen, either up for the match or
anxious to meet somebody from home,' I said. 'Some of them
must be terribly lonely; the only way they keep in touch is through
the dances.'

'Yes,' Eileen said scanning the hundred or so advertisements,
'and the other dances are for cliques too – there's the Dublin Master
Victuallers, the Master Butchers' Association, the Hairdressers'
Association, the Master Tailors, and they have all the dance halls
sewn up between the lot of them.' She reeled off the names of the
halls: 'The Balalakia in Granby Row, the Teachers' Hall in Parnell
Square, the CYMS in Harrington Street, and here's the Adelaide, it
says "no jitterbugging" allowed.'

'There's a *céilí* advertised for Barry's Hotel, with a free bicycle
park, and it says refreshments are at moderate prices.' Betty was
peering over her shoulder.

'*Céilís* are the best fun,' Eileen said. 'At least you're not expected
to have a partner for a *céilí.* Everybody can dance around together,
and you never know who you'll meet.'

'That's for the country crowd,' I said, 'and anyway Mam wouldn't
allow me that far into town for a *céilí.*'

My mother's socialising took place within her own family of
Wicklow cousins. Invitations were handed out casually, and hooleys
were really an extension of the 'rambling house' they had all been
used to in their childhood. There didn't have to be a reason for a
party, except as we grew older and it became the fashion to celebrate
twenty-first birthdays. My mother encouraged us to bring our
friends to the house. Madge and Babs, who were involved in a mixed
presidium of the Legion of Mary and had lots of friends both male
and female, were great for organising get-togethers. My mother joined
in the preparations with great energy and was always considered a
member of the party. My grandfather, who in his day lived for family

gatherings, would have looked in disgust at the elegant displays which Madge and Babs prepared for their Saturday evening parties. He would have reached for his pipe, clamped it between his teeth, and begun muttering about the vagaries of the younger generation.

Tinned John West salmon, absent from grocery shops during the war, was swimming once again; spread liberally on halves of Bewley's finger-rolls, it made a sophisticated change from the hearty thick cheese wedges of my grandfather's day. Newfangled sliced pans were popular; filled with ham they were cut in delicate triangles to sit like waves on a seashore. Squeezing thick pork sausages out of their skins into bite-sized pieces was a new innovation of the post-war entertaining scene. Tiny pastries, decorated sponge squares and tiny chocolate eclairs pushed the hefty wedges of fruit- cake onto the bottom plate of the three-tiered cake-stands, a number of which, collected over the years as prizes in dancing competitions, were now being put to practical use. Tea and lemonade were always served. Most young people took the pledge to abstain from alcohol on their Confirmation day and many went on to become firm members of Father Matthew's Pioneer Total Abstinence Association. My mother and those of her generation were brought up where drink was enjoyed at Christmas and social occasions, so a bottle of brandy, whiskey, port wine and sherry graced every kitchen press and was offered when the occasion arose, but it was not prevalent at our parties.

Grandfather would have frowned on the party games of 'forfeits' and 'musical chairs', 'charades' and 'spin the bottle' which had replaced the chat and the ballads. He might have settled himself to listen to the recitations and the monologues which were becoming the backbone of these parties, and he might have shed a tear for mad Carew and the Colonel's daughter in the sad saga of 'The Green Eye of the Little Yellow God'. I know he would have thumped his stick and demanded 'Kevin Barry' and the ballad of Sean Tracey and Michael Dwyer, and agreed with the censor who was reported to have banned the love lyrics of 'South of the Border'. We sang and talked and did our party pieces, prolonging the night till early morning almost as if that were expected of us. Then we dragged our weary limbs and sleep-starved eyes to the first Mass of Sunday morning and declared the party a roaring success.

I was trying to persuade Patsy to come to the *céilí* in the Mansion House. Since Madge and Babs were going with their friends, it would be an opportunity for us to try it out.

'Yes or no, will you come? Somebody will leave you home,' I said. Patsy lived nearly a mile from my home, and I knew her father would be anxious about her. As soon as we agreed to go, we immediately went into a tizzy as to what we would wear.

We debated the wisdom of wearing lipstick and any other make-up. Women rarely wore make-up, and though both Madge and Babs used lipstick on occasion, I had been put off initially by somebody saying that it was made from insects' blood. I had bought my first bottle of clear nail-varnish from my first week's wages. Colourless nail-varnish was discreet, and I fancied that it made my fingers look long and slender when they flashed over the typewriter keys, but on the whole make-up was never used in the workplace; it was kept strictly for weekends. I eventually graduated to nail-varnish with a slight pink blush, but I knew that bright red would not be looked on favourably by my mother.

'I bought myself a lipstick,' I said to my mother, as I prepared for the all-important *céilí*. 'Do you want to see it?' I said, outlining a Cupid's bow on my upper lip.

'I hope it's not bright red.'

'Why don't you look?'

'It looks well,' she said, as she looked at the light pink tinge.

'You've got it plastered all over you,' Babs' remarked unkindly when she surveyed my handiwork. 'Let me show you how to do it.' She perched herself in front of the mirror with my good new lipstick in her hand.

'One thing I don't want to see any of you wearing,' my mother said, 'is pancake make-up. It looks so unreal. Your skin is good enough as it is, and that dreadful stuff must clog the pores. And definitely none of that rouge on your cheeks.'

'It'll bring you out in spots,' Betty commented as she passed into the scullery behind me.

'You're just jealous you're not going to the *céilí*,' I said to her, as I flounced rougeless up the stairs to get ready.

I didn't need rouge that evening. Before an hour was over my cheeks were flaming red from the energetic swinging, two-stepping, stamping and clapping through the Walls of Limerick, the Siege of Ennis and the Humours of Bandon, and we were thirsting for glasses of milk or orange to soothe our parched throats. As we pedalled home in a group, I knew I had had one glorious evening. This dancing was beginning to catch on.

'Are you going anywhere this evening?' my mother asked me one evening after work as I was preparing to change out of my office clothes. It was three months since the Rome trip, and the memory was beginning to fade a bit.

'Not particularly.'

'You know the O'Keeffe boys?' she said, 'I met their mother today. Her boys are planning to go to Rome and she was wondering if you could tell them a little bit about your trip.'

Of course I knew the O'Keeffe boys. They were neighbours' children, and we had played together when we were young. Their youngest sister, Peg, was Nance's friend. As we lived within a stone's throw of each other I saw the two of them regularly, usually in deep conversation with a friend who shared their cycling holidays, all three seated on their bikes. They used to give me a lofty wave when I cycled past.

I borrowed my mother's stylish new raincoat, which I rather fancied, turned the collar up in the fashion of the day and presented myself at the door of their house. Three tall, good-looking young men, all in their twenties, who had been poring over a map spread on the dining-room table, rose to their feet when I was shown in. All three were seasoned hostellers in Ireland, and the previous year they had taken their bicycles and toured the south coast of England.

'Which Channel port did you go by?' Tom, the eldest of the three, asked me. He was the one who was planning the trip. I knew he was a clerical officer in the ESB having, like myself, worked his way through the ranks.

'Newhaven-Dieppe,' I said. 'It wasn't the best of crossings. I think Dover-Calais is better.'

'That wouldn't suit us,' Tom said, consulting the map. 'Dieppe is only 100 miles from Paris and a shorter route for us with the bicycles.'

'With the what?' I said in astonishment. 'You're not thinking of cycling to Rome?' The three of them nodded. 'But it's over a thousand miles,' I croaked in disbelief.

'We'll take a train some of the way, but we'll do a lot of cycling.' They each had the regulation two weeks' holiday and an extra day for the August Bank Holiday. The balance of the three weeks they would take at their own expense, and their time would be limited to three full days in Rome. They intended to carry everything they needed on their bicycles, three all-steel Raleigh bikes with dropped handle-bars and cable brakes.

'You'll never carry that load with you,' I said as I read through the list they had drawn up. There were mess-tins, water bottles, a couple of primus stoves, tent, rain gear, changes of clothing and their long pants. They would travel in shorts, but must have their arms and legs covered to be allowed enter any of the basilicas to make the Holy Year visits.

'At least you get away with bare heads,' I said, remembering the black lace mantillas which covered the heads of the pilgrims, selections of which were now appearing in all the fashion shops.

As Tom pointed out their route to me, I thought how confident he seemed in his planning.

'You'll need lots more currency than we carried,' I said, thinking that we only had to carry pocket-money. They had to plan for money for food, trains and all expenses – sterling, French francs, Swiss francs and Italian lira – and estimate how much they would need as they crossed each frontier. We talked late into the night, while Tom's anxiously hovering mother plied us with cups of tea. They were curious about what we had seen in Rome, and they wanted to know the conditions to fulfil the Holy Year obligation. They already knew they must report to the pilgrimage office at the Vatican and get their *tesseras* and information about a papal audience. I gave them details of where to buy the 'flicking Pope', which their mother had already promised to all her friends.

I was madly jealous of the preparations they were making. Oh well, I thought, I had done what I'd been asked, and that was the end of that.

I didn't see them go on the morning of their departure, but I got up-to-date bulletins of their progress from their mother, who read out their tightly written postcards which told of how they had cycled to Paris, made it over the St Bernard Pass and finally arrived in Rome.

It was a week or so after their return before I got a first-hand report on the trip from Tom. He was back at work and already into studying at night for his secretarial exams. We met as we both turned for home from the top of Dolphin's Barn Street where we had parted company from our respective friends.

'I called, but you were out,' he said.

'I suppose my mother said I was never in.' My Guiding activities kept me flying.

'Something like that,' he grinned. I sat on the saddle of my bicycle, comfortably upright with a pedal wedged against the foot-path, while he stood astride the crossbar of his bike, easing back against the hard leather saddle to rest.

'That's a trip to remember for a long time,' I said as he told me of the things which had happened to them during their three weeks away. In Paris they camped in a football stadium which had been converted into a tented village for tourists, most of them young male university students exploring the freedom of travel through a war-ravaged Europe whose frontiers had only just opened up. I envied them their cycle along the shores of Lake Geneva. They took the hard slog over the St Bernard Pass between Switzerland and Italy and stayed in the primitive guest accommodation afforded them by the Benedictines in their monastery 8,000 feet above sea level, in the glorious scenery of the Alps. They travelled in the true spirit of the medieval pilgrim and were given free accommodation in a tented village in Rome's suburbs, in common with other youth pilgrims from all over Europe. Like ourselves, they had a religious contact in Rome, and the Irish Christian Brothers took them under their wings, fixed up a papal audience and told them where to go and what to see.

'We had a lucky break when we were leaving Rome,' Tom laughed. 'We got a lift in a lorry heading for Genoa, packed with sacks of potatoes and turnips, and the lorry driver hoisted the three bikes on the top.' Tom travelled with the bikes on top of the turnips for a day and a night as the lorry rumbled northwards, crossing temporary wooden bridges replacing those which had been destroyed by the retreating German army. They planned to take the train from Genoa to Lyons and cycle up the scenic Rhone valley to Paris. 'But we lost the bikes,' Tom said looking at the wheels of his new bicycle. 'We had to change trains in the middle of the night and we got on the Paris train by mistake; the bicycles went to Lyons.' After calling to the Irish Embassy they set off once again to a tented village, this one on a cleared bomb-site next to the Hotel des Invalides. The walls surrounding the bomb-site and the adjacent streets were clearly pock-marked by gunfire, a sober reminder of how Europe had suffered during the long years of the Second World War.

We talked for over an hour, until I suddenly realised that my mother would wonder where I was, and we unravelled our bicycle wheels and parted company.

'What kept you?' my mother said, looking at the clock. 'It's nearly eleven o'clock.'

'I bumped into Tom and he filled me in on his holiday to Rome.'

'He called earlier,' she said as she wound the alarm clock for the morning.

'Good-looking,' Nance remarked. I ignored her. If I was attracted to him, as I was, there was nothing I could do about it. He would have to make the first move. We didn't move in the same circle of friends, I told myself, considering again the disadvantage of having no brothers.

'How did you know where I worked?' I motioned frantically to Noreen on the switchboard, who still held her line as I spoke into the telephone. She reluctantly cut herself off.

'I trailed you the other day,' Tom answered. Full marks for initiative, I thought.

'I have tickets for the opera in the Gaiety.'

'What's on?' I said, stalling for time.

'*Rigoletto*,' he said. 'It will be a party of four if you'll come.' I paused long enough not to sound too eager, and accepted.

'Well,' Noreen said from her desk by the switchboard, 'who was it?'

'Mind your own business,' I grinned as I clipped the receiver from the dictaphone onto my ears and stared out over Trinity

College. I suddenly remembered Brother Michael and the morning in Michaela's in Rome.

'Going somewhere special?' my mother enquired a few days later as I vaselined my best patent leather shoes, shot rags with a spray of setting lotion into my long straight hair and brushed it gently half an hour later into a page-boy curl on my shoulder.

'To the opera,' I said as casually as I could.

'Oh. On the bike?' she asked, equally casually, as she surveyed the preparations.

'No.' She knew there wasn't much point in probing further.

Tom was waiting for me across from Dolphin's Barn Church, and presented me with a large box of Black Magic chocolates, the doyen of chocolates since the ending of the war. He was slim and handsome in a dark grey suit, with a maroon silk tie and floppy matching handkerchief in his breast pocket. With comfortable seats in the parterre and superb music, our first evening out had a very special quality.

Of course, everybody knew something was going on. Our homes were too close. We varied our meeting places to throw people off the scent and enjoyed the intrigue, but Patsy and Eileen and some more of my friends became suspicious when I wasn't always available for planned outings any longer.

My mother observed the shampooing, the hundred strokes with the hairbrush, the nail varnishing, the ironing and pleating of skirts with a watchful eye and waited.

'Who owns the half-empty box of chocolates in the end of the wardrobe?' Madge held the long black box high above her head. One of the drawbacks of shared bedrooms, I thought grimly as I dived for the box. The cat was firmly out of the bag now.

'I told you he was good-looking,' Nance said again to no one in particular, airily selecting a chocolate.

'Good taste too,' Betty said as she scanned the menu on the box. 'Will we be treated to these sort of luxuries every week or are they only for special occasions?'

'I knew all along,' Madge informed us.

'You were spotted,' my mother said. 'Somebody saw you walking home from town, and news travels very fast, you know.'

Thursday became our special night out, and I was reminded of the times in Parkes when we badgered Victoria about her Thursday night date. It was wages night for most salaried workers and one of the nights Tom took off from studying. We shared a love of theatre, opera and light opera, and if we failed to book seats in advance we queued up for the 'gods' in the Gaiety or the Olympia.

'A dress dance!' I said, looking at the tickets Tom had placed in my hands, not believing my eyes. It was a Friday night, one of his study nights, and we hadn't been supposed to meet.

'They came through today. I ordered them last week and I wanted to tell you as soon as possible. I meant this to be a pleasant surprise,' he finished lamely as I looked dumbly at the two dance tickets in my hand.

'They are a wonderful surprise,' I said, looking up and wanting to hug him on the spot, which would have given the neighbours something to talk about. 'I've never been to a dress dance.'

'That makes two of us,' Tom said. 'There's a group going from the office and they invited us to make up the party.' I looked at the date and saw that it gave me a month to plan a dress. A dress dance with all its glamour and excitement would be worth ten dances in the Crystal or the Olympic ballrooms. I was hopping with excitement by the time I got in the door. I whirled around the kitchen.

'All the dating is gone to her head,' Betty volunteered as she made room at the tea table.

'I'm going to the Metropole to a dress dance.'

'That's really doing things in style,' Nance said. 'The Metropole Ballroom no less.' The Metropole with its gleaming foyer and glittering lights had been a fairyland to us as children when we were taken during the Christmas holidays to see Shirley Temple, Jane Withers or Mickey Rooney.

'That costs a lot of money,' my mother said, practical as usual.

'That's not her worry,' Madge said. 'Her worry is her dress.'

'It will be full formal dress,' I explained to my mother, and already my mind was away with visions of tulle and satin, 'and there'll be a formal dinner and a full band.'

'And it goes on until two or three o'clock in the morning,' Betty threw in.

'How will you get there in your full formal dress?' my mother wanted to know.

'By taxi, there and back,' I told her. Taxis, as far as my mother was concerned, were the height of extravagance, and a big black taxi arriving for me would cause no end of comment. She mused on all this extravagance as she moved between the kitchen and the scullery.

'You don't go on the bus to a dress dance,' Betty hooted, 'but I know somebody who went on his bike with his girlfriend on the back because the taxi got lost.' Everybody ignored her.

'Does Tom have to pay for all this?' my mother asked.

'Of course,' we chorused. She stared at us in disbelief. Married at twenty-one, she had never been to a dance, except to family weddings when her dancing would have been confined to taking part in a half-set. 'He pays for the tickets, the hire of his dress suit and the taxi.'

'And he must bring a flower for your shoulder,' said Tess, no doubt thinking of the romantic pictures she had seen at the cinema.

'The dress will cost me a small fortune,' I said in self-defence. A woman offering to share the cost of a night out would be an insult to any escort. Men earned higher salaries and were expected to pay for all expenses. 'That's the way things are nowadays,' I summed it up. 'It's the gentleman's privilege to look after a lady.'

I had my own ideas about what I wanted to wear. I would be meeting some of Tom's friends for the first time, and I wanted him to be proud of me. It was a worrying time, fingering tulles and laces, satins and taffetas, and wondering how to shape them into the dress of my dreams.

'It's possible to hire a dress,' Noreen in the office said when I brought in yet another sample of material. I had nearly enough pieces now, my mother pointed out, to make a small patchwork quilt.

'You're dithering,' she said. 'Settle down and decide on one thing at a time, the pattern, the material and the colour.'

As usual she was right. But I could never be satisfied with a simple pattern. It had to be complicated by borrowing a skirt design from one and twisting and turning another until I was sure of the shape of the top. I refused to have any glitter on the dress, even though the fabric shops trailed sparkling, sequin-studded net across their windows. The finest of wine-coloured tulle over pink net over pink moiré taffeta topped two underskirts of taffeta and scrim. My mother's sewing machine seemed to eat miles of pink and wine-coloured thread.

'I hate this machine,' I shouted in frustration when the long shuttle of the bobbin jammed and spewed out knots of thread and my right wrist began to take on a mind of its own as it wheeled and spun and cranked the handle on the old machine.

'You're too anxious,' my mother said as she rescued a mountain of tulle from mutilation. 'Take it easier than that. Maybe you should have taken the material to a proper dressmaker.'

The Singer Sewing Machine Company in Grafton Street saved the day. They looked at the relic of oul' dacency and rooted among discarded boxes until they found me a replacement bobbin, and work on the dress began to make steady progress.

Panic set in when the question of evening shoes came up. Nobody owned evening shoes and nobody was prepared to pay the high prices demanded for little slippers of strapped silver or gold. In the end I sacrificed my newest sandals and Tom painted them with a tiny tin of silver paint from Woolworths. I borrowed Eileen's evening bag to match the shoes, a glitzy silver-spangled purse belonging to her mother, and treated myself to an exquisite lace handkerchief which I sprayed with mine, and Tom's, favourite perfume, Goya's Gardenia.

Everyone stayed home to watch on the night of the dance; two of Tess's friends even came over to await the glamour. Disaster nearly struck when the twenty-two-inch zip on the back of the dress locked on an errant piece of thread and refused to budge, but Babs, with stoic calm, prodded and unpicked it while I primped in the mirror and adjusted the diamante earrings I had purchased at the last minute in Woolworths. Then the lace elbow-length gloves went missing. I had trawled nearly every shop in Dublin to get the exact shade I wanted and then put them away so carefully that I couldn't remember where.

Tom arrived in the taxi, looking at least six inches taller in the jet-black dinner suit, with a sprig of pink carnations for my shoulder in his hand. I looked at my mother, and she nodded. He had asked her what colour to buy.

'Wear your jacket,' she said, handing it to Tom who draped it around my shoulders as to the manner born. 'It's chilly tonight.' But I felt no chill as I dipped my head and settled my dress around me in the taxi.

'Are you sure you've got room for me,' Tom asked as he looked at the skirt spread on the seat. He took my hand as we rode proudly to the city, where we joined Frank and Padraig and their girlfriends under the great canopy of the Metropole. No film star got more attention than we did. We were met with flashing bulbs from opportunist photographers who grabbed us and filmed us and hounded the boys for orders. The liveried doorman held the great glass doors wide and swept our grandeur through with an extravagant gesture.

We slowly ascended the staircase, lifting the long skirts in both hands like practised debutantes, hoping that the jackets carelessly slung on our shoulders would stay balanced. Confident and graceful, we were being escorted by the three handsomest men in the city that night, their faces tightly shaved, unruly hair tamed with hair-tonic, resplendent in the hired dinner-jackets, stiff winged collars, flowing white silk scarves and shoes polished till they gleamed.

In the cloakroom we assessed each other's finery, straightened each other's glittering paste jewellery, lent a hand to fluff out stubborn curls and tested and touched up lipstick and powder. With skirts held at one side at just the right angle to avoid tripping, we joined our partners on the maple-sprung floor. Each had eyes for his own partner only, and we were swept in a close embrace into the romance and strains of a slow waltz. Tom was a sure dancer and guided me safely through the steps of the waltzes and quick-steps, and his arm was firmly there when my feet slipped as we attempted the dangerous turns of the rumba and tango on the polished floor.

The lights danced in prisms on the walls and elegant coping of the ceiling, mingled on a sea of blues, yellows, pinks and whites from the gowns of the dancers, bounced off the silver and brass of the instruments and spot-lit the drummer as he crescendoed each selection to a close. Spot prizes had been donated by the sponsors: gold cartons of Will's or Player's cigarettes, bottles of spirit and festive boxes of chocolates and perfumes. The master of ceremonies thought up competition gimmicks, and partners whooped and swooped, searching for used tram tickets, a pawn-ticket, a lady's size three shoe, a set of braces or a gold earring.

Exuberant spirits, reluctant to let the night drift away, dragged tired feet into the long ribbon of La Conga as dancers gripped each other's waists and snaked around the ballroom, weaving in and around the supper tables, now strewn with half-empty glasses, opened boxes of chocolates, discarded gloves and wilting corsages.

To lull us back to the romance of the evening, the lights were dimmed and the music slowed and muted. Couples swayed to the strains of the 'Tennessee Waltz', 'Over the Waves' and the 'Blue Danube', heads close together, sketching slow, dreamy steps. As the night ticked inexorably away, the spell was broken and flagging bodies pulled to stiff attention for the playing of the National Anthem.

It was the afternoon of the early morning after the night that had been when sleep eventually caught up with me, and I nodded drowsily over squiggles of shorthand as they leered and pranced across the dancing lines of my office notebook.

13
Decisions

'IS EVERYBODY CLEAR on the arrangements for Sunday?'

'Yes, Captain,' they chorused back at me.

'Please, Captain, me Mammy wants to know will we be stopping somewhere on the road.'

'For what?' The child's eyes dropped in confusion and there were giggles all round. Ah well, I'd walked myself into that one.

'Tell your Mammy we'll be stopping somewhere for you to run around and stretch your legs. You're not to worry.'

When I was commissioned as an officer in my twenty-first year, I had already been running the company for four years on a 'temporary' basis. My company wanted to be part of everything that came up, and their activities kept me on my toes. They were as big a part of my life as I was of theirs, but a tension was beginning to creep in. Having arranged an outing in the freshness and enthusiasm of Monday's meeting, I would twist and turn on the Saturday night as I visualised the dangers of adventurous feet climbing rocks in some place like the Powerscourt Waterfall and falling into the foaming water below.

'The most worrying part of it all,' I tried to explain to Tom, 'is that the parents trust me to bring each and every one safely and soundly home.'

'And you will, you know,' he reassured me. 'You always have.'

Tom was a large part of the reason for my present difficulties. He and I had a common interest in cycling and hill-walking which we shared with some of his friends, and when I didn't always have a weekend free to go hiking with the Guides, I could sense the grumbling. Although Tom and I both had loyalties which had built up over the years, it was inevitable that we would draw away from them as we became closer to each other.

Early in the summer I arranged a visit to Mount Saint Joseph Abbey, a Cistercian monastery near Roscrea in County Tipperary. I had visited the monastery with my mother some years previously. She had heard of it from a friend and loved the little walks, the millstream, and the peace of the monastery church. For the four or five days she spent there each year, she took a large bag of knitting or crotchet and contentedly spent her time eating good plain monastic food and sleeping in the ladies' guest-house outside the monastery gates; there was a guest-house for men within the monastery walls.

Cistercian monasteries have a tradition of hospitality to the traveller, and people came to the abbey from far and near to rest, to recuperate from serious illness or simply to savour the peace and serenity of the rule of silence and prayer. Whenever we visited the monastery we took the train to Roscrea and walked the two miles to the ladies' guest-house, dragging our cases until the spire of the monastery church, like a sharp needle pointing to Heaven, emerged through the surrounding trees. For me the initial boredom of long hours with nothing to do but read, walk and read again gradually gave way to a lethargic acceptance of the peace, the solitude and the silence, so that each time I left its gates it was with regret and a firm resolve to return.

I thought it would be wonderful for city kids to experience something of that calmness and quiet, to discover a little about farming and the countryside, for the abbey kept a well-tended farm on its land, and of course to learn about the lives of the monks. But as I finalised the last details with the patrol leaders, I had to force myself to concentrate. A dreadful uncertainty hung over the all-important trip.

'I couldn't tell them,' I said anxiously to Tom when he called for me after the meeting.

My mother and Tom's were part of a group of mature women who did Legion of Mary work once a week in a hostel for single mothers and their children on the north side of the city. On the previous Wednesday, having walked home from the hostel, she complained of feeling unwell. The doctor we called admitted her to hospital where she suffered a serious coronary attack. She had just passed her fiftieth birthday. Time stood still for all of us as, numb with shock and disbelief, we drew closer together as if to shield each other from what might be the inevitable and kept the house going under a thin veneer of normality.

The news remained bad all that week. Visits to my mother's bed were strictly curtailed. On Saturday night, Uncle Tom, my father's brother, arrived from visiting my mother, his face downcast. For a long time he sat on the sofa in the parlour with his head in his hands, and then startled us all by dropping to his knees and fishing his rosary beads out of his pocket.

'Get down on your knees,' he said. 'We'll pray for your mother.' Seeing a grown man cry was the most upsetting thing of all. We sobbed our way through the Rosary.

'I'll cancel tomorrow's trip,' I said to Madge, late into that dreadful Saturday night.

'She had her heart set on your going,' she said, 'and all those children were depending on you.' My mother had been as excited and pleased as my Guides by the proposed trip to Roscrea.

'They'll get over it,' I muttered, at the same time dreading cancelling all the arrangements. If I felt it had to be done, *I* would do it; it wasn't something I would ask one of my friends to undertake for me. But by dawn on Sunday morning, I had determined that the trip would not go ahead if my mother's life were still in danger.

Tess, Nance and I cycled to the hospital at seven o'clock, already dressed in our uniforms, and hoping we would impress the porter. He was flabbergasted.

'You what? Nobody is allowed in a corridor at this hour of the morning, much less in a hospital ward,' he said in disbelief as he barred our way.

'I thought it was all go since six o'clock,' I replied tartly. Tess punched me in the side and melted the porter with a sweet smile. She explained that my mother was very ill and we wanted to know how she had passed the night.

'I'll enquire,' he said doubtfully, 'but it's Sunday morning and the doctors haven't been on their rounds yet.'

'I'd like to see the sister on the ward.' I knew that he hadn't grasped the importance of a Guide trip waiting to be cancelled and the need for haste. He looked at me and saw I was not going to budge. Five minutes later the night sister on duty bustled briskly through the glass doors to face three very anxious daughters unwilling to leave an ailing mother who, if the predictions of the previous week came true, might die at any time.

'Leave it with me,' she said, her starchy manner relaxing. Her smiling face on her return unnerved the three of us, and tears sprang quickly to our eyes.

'She's had a comfortable night,' she said. 'I've just spoken to the consultant, and he considers your mother is out of danger.'

'You're not . . .' I began.

'No,' she said, 'I'm telling you the truth. She turned the corner round midnight. What's more,' she said, 'you can see for yourself.' An astonished porter watched as she escorted us to our mother's ward. This was unheard of in a Dublin hospital.

'No,' Sister said, 'you may not go in. I've told her you're on your way for your day's outing, and just dropped in as you were passing the hospital. She knows she has been very ill, but I don't want to alarm her.'

Through the open door of the ward we waved and my mother mouthed one word, 'GO!' We went. My mother had no intention of relinquishing her hold on life and her family just yet.

'She'll be proud of your concern,' Sister said gently. 'Any mother would.'

As the bus entered the monastery gates, a silence fell on forty young voices. I had explained about the monks, their life and the history of the order from the rule of St Benedict through the glorious days of St Bernard of Clairvaux, but the sight of a monk in his habit of black and white, with the hood closely hugging his face and his eyes downcast, indicating that he must not speak or be spoken to, brought the reality of monastic life home to them. Undeterred, they poured out of the bus, swarmed up the small rise and into the trees, leaving the calm serenity of the monastery trembling in their wake.

The monks did us proud with the huge lunch they spread for forty hungry youngsters, who chattered their heads off and helped stack the plates and carry them to the kitchen, vieing with each other to wash up. They were keen to see everything, to find out all about the monks, to be shown everything in the enclosure. I brought them to the flour mill where I had on other days watched the brothers measure and weigh the grain and mill their own flour. Gentle, white-haired Brother Vincent, brother of the Abbey Theatre's Sara Allgood, saw his repository shelves laid bare as eager fingers sought for medals and holy pictures to bring home as souvenirs. Forty inquisitive faces craned on straining necks to see over the screen separating the cloister from the public chapel and listened with rapt attention to the chanting of the monks.

Permission was given for Brother Matthew to join us for an impromptu concert. A special friend of my mother and a neighbour from Cork Street, he had worked in Guinness's Brewery before answering the call to the monastic life, far from Dublin's busy streets. The guest-master and Brother Columba also joined in while more monks hovered uncertainly in the background, and our solos, duets and choruses from Gilbert and Sullivan, hiking and company camp-songs delighted the monks and kitchen staff.

At the doors of the bus we regrouped, and in the calm silence of a Sunday evening we ended the day. It was a solemn moment as forty young voices sang,

'Day is done, gone the sun
From the hills, from the lakes, from the sky,
All is well, safely rest,
God is nigh.'

The driver hooted his horn in farewell, and the monastery settled back into silence. Tonight in the darkness of the cloister, before the lighted halo of the Virgin's statue, when the haunting strains of the *Salve Regina* had been sung, the monks would pray for our safe journey and remember my mother in their prayers.

Time was marching on and my Guides were blossoming into young adults. Now past fourteen years of age and expected to leave childhood behind them, they were working in factories, offices or shops. Twenty-first birthday parties were looming for the older ones, and a few had lined up boyfriends. The pattern of my own life was changing too.

Proud possessors of bicycles, my company was anxious to go further afield, and we agreed to go cycling to the Scalp near Enniskerry in County Wicklow the following Saturday. Conscious all the time of increasing traffic as we cycled two abreast through Dundrum and past Stepaside, I felt I had earned my laze in the sunshine when we eventually stopped. I closed my eyes while activity hummed around me.

'Ellen has fallen, Captain.'

I should have used the eyes in the back of my head, I thought. I scrambled up the path to the rocks where she had fallen, her right ankle twisted beneath her. We carried her in an armchair of arms, stumbling along the path to the bicycles. The nearest public phone was back at Dundrum village or further on to Enniskerry, nearly two miles either way. The nearest ambulance was at the Meath Hospital. I thanked God the injury wasn't more serious.

'I'll take her on the back-carrier of my bike,' I said to Patsy, who came on excursions to help me out. 'You get the rest of them together and see them safely home.' I wasn't sure whose task was the hardest. Ellen's bicycle couldn't be left at the Scalp; none of the parents had a car to collect it.

'I'll take the two bikes,' Nancy, one of my senior patrol leaders and a tower of strength, said in her imperturbable way. 'I've done it before.'

Ellen gripped my waist as we swung into the Enniskerry road, and Nancy steered her own bike with one hand as she propelled the second bike beside her. When we stopped just outside Stepaside village to rest, a sympathetic motorist, noticing the huddle at the side of the road, stopped, hoisted the two bicycles into his capacious boot and drove us both to the hospital.

In the quiet of the casualty ward at the Meath Hospital, I remembered I had arranged to meet Tom that evening, and I still had to get Ellen safely home. As I leaned back on the wooden form lining the casualty waiting-room the decision wasn't hard to make. I would write my resignation next week. I had paid my dues.

My resignation from the Guides was the give-away, and everybody waited with bated breath to hear the announcement of an engagement.

'Did you get a watch for Christmas, Captain?' The cheeky grin halted me as I was signing the company log for the last time. 'Let's see.' Before I could move, my wrist was held firm and the cuff flicked back to reveal my old black-strapped watch still in its usual place.

'Sorry to disappoint you,' I said and bent to conceal the giggle I was trying to suppress.

'We'll keep them guessing,' I had said to Tom. The decision to quit Guiding had been all mine and had a lot to do with needing freedom to do my own thing. Of course, there was something in the wind, but we weren't about to announce a wedding day yet, even though we were planning one. Neither of us liked the convention of a long engagement, the ritual of the presentation of a gold watch to indicate that a proposal of marriage was in the offing and as the signal for starting a 'bottom drawer', with birthday and Christmas presents bought with a marriage label attached. I wanted to be free of expectations and limitations.

'Tom,' I ventured one day when we were cycling past the gate of the Carmelite Convent in Ranelagh, heading for the beach at Seapoint, 'would you come to see Jennie with me? She asks about you, because little birds have been whispering, and she'd love to see you again.'

'You visit Jennie quite a bit,' Tom said.

'On and off. Patsy and I go, but we never see her. She talks to us from behind a curtain.'

We pedalled on in silence. The pull of the convent was weakening, but I realised that, yes, I was reluctant to let the idea go. I glanced at Tom and his face was serious. Had I ever truly considered a religious calling, the prospect of spending my life within the confines of a convent? I knew I didn't have the courage and single-mindedness of Jennie; I knew it surely now as I glanced once again at Tom.

'Race you to the corner,' I said as I took off up the Ranelagh Road. His hand on my shoulder pulled me back.

'The Lord never called me,' I said as he drew alongside.

Next evening I scanned the *Evening Mail* spread flat on the kitchen table, muttering away to myself as I read.

'What are you nattering about?' my mother said from her chair by the fire. She had received a clean bill of health from the hospital, though she was told to take things a little easier.

'Just having some fun,' I said, 'just seeing how many jobs I should be applying for. There's half-a-dozen here which are very attractive; there's even one offering an opportunity to travel.'

'I thought you had your mind on other things,' she said soberly, 'and I can't see travel fitting into that scene.' Nor could I. I sat back contentedly, contemplating what I hoped would be a better future: the exciting prospect of building my own home with Tom and planning our life together, one in which there would be no place for exciting, exacting jobs with prospects of travel. After Miss Feeney's remarks I had occasionally allowed myself the luxury of thinking about a legal career and studying for the law, but I knew in my heart that it was out of the question. Financially and from an educational point of view, it simply wasn't possible. Instead I would become a full-time wife and homemaker, and my working life outside the home would come to an end. The realisation began to dawn on me that I would be dependent on Tom for all my needs for the rest of my life.

Thinking of marriage also reminded me of how much I would miss my father on that day. When my father was alive he never missed a Gaelic football semi-final or final, and now Tom and I cycled across to the north side of the city, locked our bicycles in the pile outside Croke Park and clambered through the stile to join the crowds on Hill 16. These were the days when I remembered my father most and felt sad that he would not be there to support me and give me away on my wedding day.

Far from leaving a void in my life, as I had feared it might, resigning from the Guides left me with time to broaden my horizons. My friends were still there. I had actually poached two of the more senior Guides, Mary and Laura, from their own jobs and persuaded them to work with me in College Green. I had also made a very close friend, Deirdre, who had joined the firm a year or so previously when we needed an extra pair of hands and she needed a job. She had little office and no legal experience, and it was my job to initiate her in the workings of a law firm. She quickly grasped the rules by which an out-of-date legal system dictated our every move. Staples must never be used on original documents. Wills must be folded in a certain manner, and other documents must be folded in a regulation two or four folds. Assignments and leases were typed on parchment paper, contracts and agreements on thick 'Judy' or Judicature paper, and documents hand-sewn with a large-eyed darning needle, using green tape or cord. She picked it up in no time at all.

Deirdre's experience stretched far beyond the narrow confines of daily office routine. Endowed with a gifted speaking voice, she had deserted a normal career in favour of treading the boards. Her long straight hair cut in a fringe framed a gamin, Audrey Hepburn-like face, and her arresting voice had heads turning in our direction when we entered a café for a cup of tea, a fact of which Deirdre was totally unaware.

'Ireland is my adopted country,' she was fond of declaring. She visited her grandmother in County Cork frequently, and brought us back boxes of Hedji Bey's wonderful homemade Turkish delight. A Yorkshire lass, she loved her native county where her mother, a doctor, still lived and practised. Deirdre had worked with repertory companies in England, and toured for a while with Anew MacMaster's company here, and her accounts of life in a touring theatre fascinated all of us. She was a free spirit, living a life of independence which I, in my own way, envied. Everybody in the office lived at home, as all Dublin people did, and we thought she took enormous risks by living on her own in a flat near the centre of the city.

We met one evening a week for a meal at her flat. I would bring tiny cakes and she cooked meals of fried bananas with bacon and eggs, followed by battered apple-rings. We shared an enthusiasm for the flattest shoes we could find, and she would rush in from her lunch-hour, hair flying and eyes popping, to tell me that Dolcis or Tylers in Grafton Street had a new style in. She pined at times for her only sister Rachel, who had married a Yorkshire man and gone to share a new life with him in South Africa, further away than any of us could imagine, and we shared her worries, joys and anxieties when Rachel's letters arrived.

We also shared an interest in theatre and loved to compare notes on the various performances we saw, particularly those at the Gate

Theatre which housed some of Anew MacMaster's productions. It was Lord Longford's boast that a couple could have a night out at the Gate for half-a-crown; the wooden seats at the back of the small theatre were great value at one shilling each and the programme cost the enormous sum of sixpence. Most of my theatre-going was now with Tom, but Deirdre had other friends to go with, and we mused with Michael MacLiammóir in *Ill-Met by Moonlight* and enjoyed the viciousness of Coralie Carmichael in Chekhov's chilling *Three Sisters*.

We became familiar with the names and faces who populated Dublin's theatre world, as our enthusiasm brought us from the Gate and the Abbey to the tiny Pike Theatre in Herbert Street. Like all of Dublin, I was fascinated by the suave, expressionless face of Hilton Edwards, and amazed at the posturing of MacLiammóir, who carried his careful make-up from the stage into everyday life. I loved Anna Manahan for her sincerity in every part she played, gentle Sally Travers, niece of MacLiammóir, Paddy Bedford, who was a neighbour's grandchild from Dolphin's Barn Street, and Christopher Casson, whose quiet cultured voice reached to every corner of the theatre. Tom and I went to the first performance of Maura Laverty's *Liffey Lane*, and I cried at the sadness and dereliction to be found in an old man's soul. We followed Des Keogh and Rosaleen Linehan in their revues in Bus Áras and sat through MacLiammóir's *Hamlet* in the Olympia and *Everyman* in the Capital Cinema, converted to a theatre for this wonderful production. Or we might have a night at the Abbey, with perhaps May Craig and Eileen Crowe, Jack MacGahern, Milo O'Shea, Cyril Cusack, Harry Brogan and the solid, sensible faces of the Golden brothers.

It was the feeling of being part of a special night out which lured us from the cinema queues. At the theatre we were part of a big party. During the interval, even though we might know nobody else there, we rubbed shoulders with actors and distinguished guests all dressed for an evening's entertainment. We dressed for the occasions too, Tom in his best suit and crombie overcoat, me with a theatre stole draped over my best blouse and skirt. We smiled as we placed pennies in the bowl of the 'Beggar at the Gate', as *Dublin Opinion* had nicknamed Lord Longford, who stood on the steps leading to the foyer with Lady Longford, a slight, anxious figure, hovering in the background.

The climax of our theatre outings was always supper at the Berni Inn, close to O'Connell Bridge, where unescorted ladies were not admitted. Ironically, here I was made to feel, as a swallow-tailed waiter sprang to divest me of my coat, that women were the most important people in the world. The restaurant was long and narrow and a contrast to the cosy tea-and-cakes atmosphere of the Monument Creameries and the Capitol restaurant where Tom and I could sit for hours over a plate of creamed mushrooms on toast. When I supped at the Berni Inn, I held up my head and walked two inches taller.

'Are you planning to holiday with Tom this year?' Patsy asked when we met for tea. These teas would have to be cut out shortly, I thought, if Tom and I were serious about saving. I looked at Patsy.

'You mean go away together?'

'I didn't mean that,' she said hastily. 'Will you take holiday time together and stay in Dublin?'

'No,' I said. The prospect of spending our two precious holiday weeks kicking our heels in Dublin didn't appeal to either Tom or me, and going away together was completely out of the question.

'How about a cycling holiday around Donegal?' I suggested. 'Tom is planning to go to Scotland with three of his friends.'

Patsy and two other friends who had been to Rannafast Gaeltacht were longing to visit Donegal again, and go on to Northern Ireland. Tom helped us plan the trip, but I would be away for his birthday, and this year I felt a card through the post would not be enough.

'If I record a message, will you make sure it's delivered?' I asked my mother. She clearly thought I was mad or rolling in cash, and declared she had never heard such nonsense.

'Do you make very small records?' I said to the young man sitting in a recording studio on the corner of Suffolk Street.

'How small?'

'Just a short poem. A birthday greeting,' I added hastily. He shut me into a tiny, sound-proofed room at the top of the building and watched me though a window while I self-consciously spoke my poetic greeting into the microphone. He made no comment, which was just as well, when he handed over the recorded disc of wax on a paper-thin aluminium circle. My mother, true to her word and satisfied that the recording hadn't cost me a load of money, delivered the envelope so that Tom could hear my voice on his birthday while I was miles away in the Antrim hills.

Money seemed to be on my mind all the time now as Tom and I spent another winter saving all we could. 'I can't afford it,' was my constant refrain.

'At least, try it on,' Deirdre insisted as we stood looking into Newell's fashion shop at the corner of Grafton and Chatham Streets.

'I can't afford it,' I said automatically as I looked again at the sky-blue woollen suit on the model in the window. It was beautiful, I had to admit, and just what I needed to chase the winter blues away.

'Come on,' she said as she piloted me through the shop doors. It served me right, I reminded myself; I was the one who had asked Deirdre to come with me and just look, and I had said *look*, at the suit in the window. Deirdre had other thoughts.

'It's perfect,' she said when I fitted it on. I did like the prim, collar-buttoned-to-the-neck 'dressmaker' look of the jacket and the slim straight skirt. I knew in my heart I was weakening.

'I'm getting married in a year's time,' I protested. 'We need every penny we can save.'

'You only live once,' Deirdre said stoutly, 'and you can't appear in dowdy clothes for the next twelve months. Think of all the places you can wear it to.'

Of course I gave in, and the suit was folded into a cardboard box lined with sheets of flimsy tissue paper. I was apprehensive about showing it to my mother; pale blue wasn't exactly a practical colour, and I thought she would consider the price prohibitive. To my surprise and delight she approved and nodded appreciatively each time I stepped out in it. I treated myself to a long-handled promenade umbrella and white gloves, but no hat this time. An air of change was blowing through fashion and my coloured berets were gathering dust on top of the wardrobe. Clothes were becoming more colourful and casual, although the formality of gloves with every outfit still stood.

'Will you come to Rome with me?' Deirdre said out of the blue one night as we were talking in her flat. Her request took me completely off guard since we had never contemplated a holiday together. I couldn't visualise her cycling or hostelling.

'Don't tempt me,' I wailed. This was temptation on a big scale and my heart was urging me to throw caution to the winds. 'We could do it the year after next maybe,' I said vaguely.

'It'll probably be too late then,' she said quietly. It probably would, I thought, but paid no attention to her remark beyond assuming that she was probably thinking that Continental trips for Tom and me would take a back seat once we married.

Tom and I had agreed that we would not announce our engagement until we knew where we were going to live. In the normal course of events, most couples rented their first home. Through my work in the conveyancing part of the office, however, I was aware that something new was happening in housing in Dublin.

Under a Small Dwellings Acquisition Act, the government was offering first-time buyers a grant of £285 to help with deposits on houses, and Dublin Corporation was offering loans to suitable candidates with an acceptable level of income. The area of the new house must not exceed one thousand square feet, which was fine by us.

There was a sudden proliferation of public utility societies; builders and white-collared workers, mostly civil servants, began forming themselves into limited companies to build good quality housing at reasonable prices for themselves and their members. Dublin's new housing mania had started, and Tom and I were starry-eyed at the prospect of buying our own home.

'We've nothing to lose by looking,' Tom said.

'And maybe everything to gain.' Armed with all the information I could glean in the office, Tom and I spent Sunday after Sunday on the house-hunting trail. It had nearly become a national pastime. Not only Dublin people, but also young people from the country working in Dublin dragged parents and families to the new sites and in and out of show-houses as builders and jerry-builders scrambled to acquire acres of land and compete with each other in designs, locations and proposed amenities. Architects and solicitors danced their way to the bank as the weekend trawl around the suburbs of the city yielded rich rewards.

'What are you two up to?' my mother asked, seeing our mud-caked shoes when we arrived one Sunday for tea. We had spent the afternoon sloshing through muddy cuttings and stumbling over enormous cables in an area where less than a year earlier we had hiked and picnicked. Fields around the city were now warrens of foundations, little streams we loved had disappeared into ugly concrete pipes, and the rickety stiles we had climbed on our walks were ruthlessly cut aside.

'We were looking at some new houses,' I said, looking to Tom for support.

'You're not even engaged,' my mother said, fixing us both with a serious look.

'We will be when we make a decision on a house.' Tom decided it was time to make a commitment of his honest intentions to my mother.

'Please, Mam,' I pleaded, 'don't say anything to anyone. We'd like to get the house sorted first.'

Eventually Tom rang me with the news that he was eligible for a Dublin Corporation loan. Now the hunt for a house was on in earnest.

As our search continued, we saw the countryside of south County Dublin being swallowed up. Large houses which had been landmarks for us on trips outside the city were bulldozed to make way for rows of dwellings, all small enough to come within the Act. Ribbons of concrete roads twined across verdant fields.

'You'll be miles from home,' my mother said when we told her we had put a deposit on a house in the little hamlet of Churchtown. 'It's away out in the country.'

'It smells so different out here,' Tom's brother said when we took him to see the location of the new house. 'You can actually smell the fresh air.'

The place we had chosen was familiar ground to us. We could cross any of three bridges spanning the river Dodder to get to it. Milltown Bridge was the one Tom would cross on his route home from work through Ranelagh; the Rathfarnham Bridge was our direct route from Dolphin's Barn, but the one we liked best was on the road from Rathgar village, a little humped-back bridge below the rise of Ardavon House, House of Studies of the Carmelite Fathers.

We had chosen to live below the gentle sweep of the Dublin hills and above a portion of the new wide Braemor Road, a road not yet functional for through traffic, so we felt assured that our houses would be the limit beyond which the building mania would not extend. We would be five miles from the city centre, four and a half miles from our old homes. There was a train station in Dundrum and a bus terminus at the Orwell Road, but for both our families, neither of whom had a car, we would not be within easy reach.

On May Day, with me wearing the engagement ring that Tom had put on my finger beneath the shadow of those Dublin hills and the key to our future home safely in Tom's hands, we sought the good wishes and blessings of our families.

Deirdre's eyes were bright as she hugged me.

'This is no time for tears,' I said as I looked at her.

Suddenly I realised that it was not the news of my engagement which was upsetting her.

'Is Rachel ill? I asked. She shook her head.

'I've something to tell you. It's good news really,' she said brightly. 'I too did some planning on Saturday.'

'You've had a proposal of marriage!' I guessed, twirling around the flat.

'I'm entering the Carmelite convent on the 8th of December.'

I halted and looked at her in amazement.

'You never said anything.' My voice seemed suddenly to falter. For one split second I felt unpredictably angry because she hadn't told me, and almost immediately I remembered the secrecy when Jennie had made her decision. So much depended on their being accepted by the community they were joining, and I slowly realised how lonely that decision-making must have been. She hadn't the support of another person like I had in Tom. This was something between her and God.

'I couldn't tell you,' Deirdre said.

'The 8th of December,' I said incredulously and selfishly; 'you won't be at my wedding.' A thought suddenly struck me.

'Is that why you wanted to go to Rome?'

'Yes,' she said.

'You'll never get there now,' I said gloomily, thinking how she would shut out the world when she entered the Carmelites.

As the news spread in the days that followed, none of us could visualise the vibrant, decisive, free-spirited, generous character we had all grown to love and respect being locked behind the walls of an enclosed convent. I did my best to be devil's advocate, but Deirdre's mind was made up. I was going to miss her and especially her support for the final weeks before my wedding, which had been arranged for the following February. As we drew nearer to our respective dates, the little things between us became very important, like our weekly teas and the small pieces of Bewley's fudge which she would wrap carefully and leave on my typewriter for me to find when I returned to the office some evenings to work overtime.

14

The Chosen Way

'TOM AND I are hitching to Lourdes,' I said to my mother as I helped her carry the dishes to the kitchen sink.

All day I'd been rehearsing how I would tell her, talking to myself as I cycled home from the office.

'We thought we would like to hitch-hike to Lourdes together before our wedding.' I didn't want to sound defiant about it, but how could I be matter-of-fact when my heart was in my mouth and my voice shook? Anyway, it was out now.

My mother continued stacking plates and cups and saucers on the wooden draining-board, not saying a word. I rushed in again.

'I . . .' My mother held up her hand.

'I know what you're going to tell me. You're going to tell me that it's Marian year, that because Tom and you are getting married on the feast of Our Lady of Lourdes . . .'

'Something like that,' I mumbled lamely.

There was a long silence while I carried plates to the dresser and she made a marathon job of cleaning the sink. She thumped the box of Vim around and shone the taps till they gleamed.

'We thought that since we were engaged now . . .'

'Being engaged doesn't give you a licence to go away on your own together,' she flashed at me.

Tom and I were a bit fed up with all the saving and we both agreed that we needed a break. The idea of hitch-hiking had been his – it was cheap and adventurous – and I had thrown in the shrine in Lourdes as the reason for our trip. That, we both knew, might not be good enough for either of our mothers.

I had expected an explosive, 'No, you're not going', from my mother. Young couples, even when they were engaged, did not go away from home together for a night or a weekend, much less on a holiday. I remembered how in the early hours of the previous New Year's Day my mother had given Tom his marching orders when we arrived home late from a friend's house, having missed the last bus and been forced to walk four miles from Templeogue. It was the accepted rule that daughters were not kept out late without the prior consent of parents, and lights stayed on in the front room and somebody was there to demand an explanation if the rules were transgressed. My father being dead, my mother lacked moral support, and had six daughters to worry about on her own. She was taking this very calmly, all things considered.

'Where will you stay?' my mother said, and I knew she was playing for time. I knew she didn't know what hitch-hiking involved, and indeed I had no experience of hitching myself.

'Tom is making all the arrangements,' I said. 'The first part of the plan is to take the boat to England and hitch rides to the French coast.'

'In what?' she said apprehensively.

'Tom knows all about it,' I said brightly. I might as well let him take some of the blame.

Madge, my eldest sister, walked into the kitchen. She looked from one to the other of us.

'Something's going on,' she said.

'Yes,' my mother answered, 'they're planning to hitch-hike to France. Another high-falutin' idea, but they seem to know what they're doing. I imagine they have it all worked out already.'

We left Dublin on the 1st of September on the night-ferry to Liverpool. I shared a cabin in the bowels of the ship with an old lady who chattered nervously for most of the journey. Tom fared better with a young Christian Brother who snored his head off all night. Next morning, courtesy of a contact and an exchange of silver, we slipped through a door into the first class section and breakfasted in style.

Under the bemused gaze of my cabin companion, who no doubt thought I was a 'fallen woman' and disbelieved my story entirely, I changed into a pair of blue denim jeans. I had left home in a skirt and short 'bloomer' jacket of brown corduroy, with my cotton dresses for Lourdes carefully rolled in newspaper to eliminate creasing in the haversack. Tom had persuaded me to buy the jeans. I needed no persuading really; I knew that they were the most sensible thing to wear, but I had concealed them at home. Jeans were not 'ladylike' and my mother had been tested enough.

We crossed the Mersey by ferry, a new experience for me, and within half-an-hour of leaving Birkenhead we had a lucky break; a taxi-driver on his way to pick up a fare outside the city responded to our thumbing. This was the life of Reilly, I thought, as I sat comfortably in the back seat, but Reilly never travelled in the lumbering truck which picked us up next. I sat squeezed in the high cabin between Tom and the driver, who swung his heavy wheel in great sweeping movements when we rounded corners.

'Glad a' the company, mate,' he told Tom. When we told him we came from Dublin I had the feeling he wasn't quite sure where that was.

'Ireland,' I said.

'Oh, Ireland, I've never been to Ireland. I go to Blackpool meself for the holidays. Ever been there?' And he launched into a full-scale account of the glories of Blackpool. We bought him a ploughman's lunch at a transport café and he sought out a mate who was taking an empty fish lorry to the docks. The narrow cab was impregnated with the smell of every fish that ever swam the English channel, and I was glad to see the back of it. We came into London on the East Indian Dock Road at the evening rush hour.

The East End of London teemed with workers making their way home on foot or standing in orderly queues for buses. I had never seen so many people rushing about; it was noisy and confusing with lorries, cars, bicycles and red London buses, Cockney and clipped English accents calling to each other and the screeching of hundreds of seagulls as they dipped and swooped overhead. From here we had to find a bus to take us to the centre of London for a connection to Maida Vale, where we had arranged to stay with a relative of mine for two nights. We patiently queued, our haversacks creating problems and a great deal of interest as we edged onto a packed bus.

We had one full day in London. It was my first experience of London's famous Underground and Tom and I clicked in and out through ticket stiles, some of them manned by women, both white and coloured (there were so many more coloured people than we encountered back home). We raced down echoing stone steps as an unreal, disembodied voice announced the trains' arrival, and I sailed with great aplomb on every escalator I could find.

I despaired of London and its noisy streets and would never have found my way around were it not for Tom, who had all the places we should see firmly etched in his mind. We couldn't see everything in one day so we settled for a glimpse of Buckingham Palace, the Tower of London and Westminster Cathedral. I marvelled at the size of London's great stores, and skipped from one to the next tormenting myself with visions of all the wonderful clothes I couldn't afford. That evening we ate in one of the Lyon's corner-houses, popular cafés which were found in every street in London. It was the first self-service restaurant I had ever been in.

I said goodbye to London with regret: the hordes of people of every nationality, the Tower-of-Babel noise, the elegance of its historic buildings and the hundred and one things I had not seen, would beckon me back some day. We stocked up on Mars bars, absent from Dublin since the Emergency, and left for the south coast. Our destination was Brighton Youth Hostel. Tom was a veteran of the Youth Hostel Association, but I found my first night in a dormitory amongst strange girls rather daunting. I might have taken a lesson from the young lady who arrived among us complete with attaché case, vanity case and carrying her best coat on a hanger, and oblivious to the other girls' grumbling she monopolised a washbasin for nearly an hour, her array of toiletries spread all around.

Finally we landed at Dieppe and set out on the road to Paris, travelling through the dry and dusty French countryside. Lorry-drivers seemed glad of our company though we knew no French and most of the journey passed in silence. We were dropped off near the centre of Paris and found the hotel where Tom and his friends had stayed four years previously. It was a narrow three-storey building behind the Opera House, with dark floral-patterned paper on the walls and ceiling, narrow stairs and no lift. My room was at the top, underneath the roof, and Tom was one flight down. When he left to get fresh bread at the bakery, I barred and bolted the door and started the primus stove, running the water in the wash-basin to camouflage its hissing sound. After a quick meal we set out in the early evening to take a stroll before turning in, both of us dead beat after our long day's travelling. Strangers in a foreign city neither of us were familiar with its streets, and coming back to our hotel in the darkness we noticed shadowy figures on the pavement. As we drew nearer my eyes took in their brightly-painted faces and exposed bosoms, the sheer black stockings they wore and their short skirts. Tom hurried me forward and knocked briskly on the door of our hotel.

'There's a brothel next door,' he whispered as we climbed the staircase.

'Was that there the last time you came?' I hissed, wondering what the three boys had been up to when they had last been in Paris.

'Do you think I would have brought you here if it was?' my self-rightous Tom demanded, 'don't be stupid.'

I double-checked the lock on my bedroom door and jammed two chairs side by side under the handle, but I didn't sleep. Every sound on the stairs had me rising on my elbow until dawn crept over the city. In the morning, Tom had to repeat our pre-arranged signal and shout in a loud whisper before I ventured to open the door.

Our accommodation was cheap and had one great advantage: on the corner stood a delicious bakery which spread the smell of hot bread all round the street, so when we had made tea in the kettle and breakfasted on buttery croissants, we set out to see Paris.

In the daylight the houses and shops in 'our' street looked down at heel but respectable and women were out doing their shopping, baskets looped over their arms filled with tomatoes, vegetables and sticks of bread. The street was quite devoid of its after-dark activity.

Tom's hobby was photography – he developed and printed his own – and everywhere we went we carried his camera and tripod with us; he seemed intent on recording all of Paris. We wandered through the Louvre, our footsteps echoing in the silence and empti-ness of the world's most famous gallery, marvelling as we paced back and forth before the renowned Mona Lisa, the enigma of that slow smile and the brooding eyes which followed our every move. We climbed the Eiffel Tower because it was expected and posed under the Arc de Triomphe, the travelling jeans discarded, in honour of

Paris, in favour of a full-skirted cotton dress. We strolled along the Champs-Élysées and picnicked romantically on the banks of the Seine, promising one another we'd return when we had more money. Later we found a secluded spot in the Luxembourg Gardens where the chairs stood invitingly empty, and had the primus gently humming when a commissionaire came heading our way, rattling the coins in his leather pouch. The primus spluttered and died as Tom grabbed it, I scooped up the picnic and we legged it, clutching the awkward tripod and our black and battered teapot.

We walked along the Left Bank in the autumn evening, then climbed the hill for Montmartre, stopping along the way outside the Moulin Rouge, fascinated by the sight of the famous theatre. It reality it looked tatty and in need of redecorating. As the city's artists took down their canvasses and folded their easels at the end of their day, Tom moved around the street, searching for the best angles to capture the scene in black and white, and I sipped coffee and looked out over the city.

I loved the scent of Paris: the aroma of freshly brewed coffee wafting from the tiny cafés and bars; the heady smell of a glowing cigar in every Frenchman's hand, which reminded me so much of Grafton Street; the cloying perfume of the women which conjured up romantic settings and discreet boudoirs. Paris in the right mood could be the most romantic city in the world.

We took the night-train to Lourdes. It filled quickly with excitable Frenchmen in tight suits and navy berets, their women-folk squeezing in beside them and poking me in the ribs with the indispensable baskets which they lodged on their knees. No sooner had they sat down than they uncovered the checked cloths, revealing wedges of bread-sticks sliced diagonally on which they dolloped slices of garlic salami. Lumps of cheese were cut expertly with a tobacco-like movement which reminded me of my grandfather; small bottles of wine were opened, and each one attended to his or her repast, with curious sidelong glances now and again at the strangers in their midst.

The train jerked and shook itself at the guardsman's whistle, the signal for the checked napkins to be shaken free of crumbs and mouths, faces and hands briefly wiped. The napkins were folded carefully around the empty wine bottles and tidied away. That part of their pilgrimage safely out of the way, our travelling companions now settled comfortably, and as the train swayed through the dark and silent French countryside the stout matrons, replete with wine and bread, crossed their hands on their baskets and closed their eyes. It was in the order of things.

After an hour the men went out to the corridor to pull at their short stubby pipes or smoke cigars. This was the opportunity I was looking for. The hard wooden seats of the train were not my idea of comfort for a long night, so we spread our two jackets along the hammock-like luggage rack and put my haversack at one end as an improvised pillow. Tom helped me to climb into the makeshift bed and not a matron's eyes opened in surprise. The jeans were earning their keep.

When I woke the Pyrenées loomed above and around me, dark and brooding in the mists of the morning. In the distance the medieval castle of Lourdes stood sentinel, dominating the town and the skyline. The train shunted into the valley and slowed as the rock of Massabiele, the focal point of this most famous of all Marian shrines, appeared on our right. Even at that ungodly hour the grotto was alight with candles. I could see a clutter of crutches and other medical aids abandoned by grateful pilgrims, hanging to the left of Bernadette's cavern in the rocks. Everyone in the carriage took rosaries from their pockets and began drawing them through their fingers and the glorious 'Avé of Lourdes' hymn sprang spontaneously from every throat, gathering in a haunting crescendo of sound as faces wearied by the long overnight journey strained to get a glimpse of the Virgin's shrine. This was one thing Tom and I were never likely to forget. Our train from Paris, laden with ordinary French men and women, had arrived at Mary's shrine.

Tom had organised accommodation with an Irish summer worker in Lourdes. She was a friend of a friend and staying with her would cost us little or nothing. That was the plan, but when we arrived in the door of the shop where Margaret worked her hand rose to her mouth in dismay.

'I'm sorry,' she said. 'I completely forgot. I honestly did.'

We stood, framed rucksacks on our backs, among the shop's dangling rosaries and serried rows of statues and souvenirs.

'So you have no room for us?' Tom said flatly.

'Some friends of my sister came last week and they're in the apartment now. It's full.' The girl was so flustered and upset I almost felt sorry for troubling her. Out of the corner of my eye I could see a well-coiffured, heavily-made up woman of about fifty taking a close interest in our conversation: I suspected she was the *madame*, the owner of the shop, and she clearly thought we were a danger to her entire stock. We were not welcome.

'Can you recommend anywhere to stay?' Tom asked, but *madame* was bearing down on us. I touched Tom on the arm.

'It's no use,' I said, 'let's get out of here before somebody has a heart attack.' We backed out of the shop as graciously as we could and walked in silence until we came to a bridge over the River Gave. Tom thumped his rucksack on the ground with such force that the primus stove swung loose and rolled away.

'We might need that before morning,' I reminded him.

We counted our French currency and travellers' cheques, and wondered if Lourdes boasted a bank which would cash them. All thoughts of visiting the grotto were forgotten. Unless we wanted to spend the night sleeping there, which we might conceivably have done if we could, we had to find accommodation somewhere.

In the end we began to anticipate the shaking heads: Lourdes was full. When we had planned this trip back in Dublin nobody had told us about the gypsies of Europe who assembled each year for the birthday of the Mother of God. They were gathered in the village in droves, swarthy men with coloured bandanas and gleaming earrings and women in coloured waistcoats from the mills of Gavarnie, their embroidered and tasselled shawls folded over startlingly beautiful dark-eyed children, and they smiled at us with friendly interest. One landlord eyed us speculatively and offered us a double bed in his tiny attic room and when we declined he shook his head sadly. We couldn't explain that going away together had been bad enough, but coming home and admitting that we had shared a bedroom was out of the question. Ireland, we felt, was so small that somebody would be sure to find out.

As I watched shawled women haggling over fish, vegetables and cheese at a market on the bank of the river, I realised that I was starving.

'I'm not tired enough,' I grumbled, 'without having to calculate every single thing I buy in kilos and French francs.' Tom wasn't listening.

'There's a youth hostel at Ste. Pé,' he said studying the handbook, 'its about ten miles away.'

'I'm not walking ten miles in the French countryside,' I said, 'and, besides, we don't know the way.'

But everyone at the bus station on the edge of town knew, and gave us multiple instructions in French, some of which we managed to interpret. We hitched our packs higher on our backs and moved on. Half-an-hour later we stood at a railway signal box about a mile beyond the town and waited as a single-deck bus ambled alongside. We hauled our packs up the steps and made our way to a seat at the back. The chatter on the bus stopped, the silence broken by the sub-dued flutter of caged wings in a wicker-basket and the clucking of a disturbed cock. It was the local bus, bringing shoppers and workers back to their village, and it was full of baskets packed with parcels of meat, sacks of vegetables and purchases bought in town. Their nodding heads and quick exchanges in French told us we were the focus of everyone's attention.

'Youth hostel?' we said to the bus driver when the bus pulled in to the village square. An enquiry barked in French brought a roly-poly passenger with a high-pitched voice to our side. She spouted some-thing we couldn't understand and then motioned for us to follow.

A small stream flowed through the village street. Women with sleeves rolled up, possing clothes on the smooth stones at the river's edge, stopped their work to watch us pass. This was something I had heard of but never expected to see. I paused and looked until Tom poked me in the ribs.

'We're in one of the remotest parts of the Pyrenées,' he said. 'They never heard of even a hand-washing machine, and the water in the river is free.'

Maybe I had expected France to be light years ahead of us; certainly I had not expected the primitive conditions which I knew still existed in isolated areas back home. The women smiled at me, shrugged their shoulders and went back to their chores. I hurried after Tom and our guide who rolled along beside him, chattering in a one-sided conversation until we reached the door of the hostel. She dived inside and reappeared with the warden who was her husband. He was small and taciturn and silenced his voluble wife with one sharp word. Disgruntled, she disappeared.

The hostel building was ugly and bare. I thought it looked down-right sinister.

'I don't like the look of this place,' I said to Tom, sticking very close to his side.

'Neither do I,' he said, 'it's not exactly the Gresham Hotel.' I kicked his shin as the warden fixed us with an unblinking stare, suspicious of what we were saying. Usually I could stare people back but he unnerved me. He checked our Youth Hostel cards. Conversation was at an all-time low.

'It's the only roof over our heads we're likely to get tonight,' Tom said as he reached for the register. The warden marched us down the corridor and stopped at a door, indicating to Tom that this was the men's dormitory.

'He's rumbled the fact that you're not my wife. Hard luck,' Tom quipped as the warden pointed at me and led us further down the long corridor. Our footsteps echoed eerily through the silent building. The women's section was in a wing on its own, a blank, unwelcoming dormitory with small windows set high near the ceiling. I flung my rucksack on the bunk nearest the door.

'Hardly the Shelbourne either,' I said, tired and close to tears. 'More like Kilmainham Jail.' Tom was as uneasy as me.

'Let's go back and check the men's section,' he said. Four of the bunks had packs laid on them.

'It looks like you've got company,' I said. He had, in the shape of Gerry and Dick whose strong Limerick accents came echoing from the front door. Two Germans followed in their wake. We quickly explained the situation.

'You're the only woman in the hostel,' Gerry guffawed, 'we checked the register.'

'I'm not sleeping back there on my own,' I said defiantly, and the four of them came with us to inspect the women's dorm.

'He's only ensuring there's no shenanigans,' Dick waved a caution-ary finger at me, but I was in no mood for banter. The Germans' knowledge of English was good, and their French was even better, so we all trooped to the warden's office to tell him that I would sleep in the room next to theirs. The warden didn't see it quite that way, and rejected the suggestion with short sharp answers. Here I was, surrounded by the cream of Irish and German manhood, and being thwarted by a miniature Napoleon. Eventually we reached a compromise: I must sleep in the room furthest away from the men, with at least two dormitories separating us. The warden wouldn't hear any further argument.

'It was an army barracks during the war,' Gerry explained when we had settled my things in the room allocated.

'During the First World War by the looks of it,' Tom said.

'You've not seen the half of it,' they told us as they piloted me out through a door in the side of the building, 'wait till you see the cooking arrangements, Phil.' Across what might at one time have been a parade ground, now overgrown with weeds and scutch grass, was the army kitchen. Nearly every window in the place was broken, a relic of the past war.

'You must be mad to think we can cook here,' I said as I looked at the rusty stoves. 'Is there somewhere we can eat in the village?'

'Nothing within an ass's roar,' Gerry said glumly. 'We've checked.'

Tom and the two Limerick lads cleared a trestle table and we spread newspapers on top. In London I had packed half-a-dozen packet soups, a novelty which was just reaching the shops, and Limerick yielded up a store of tinned beans. I had marvelled at the size of the tomatoes I had bought by the unfamiliar kilo, huge, rough-skinned and filled with succulent flesh, and they were the ideal accompaniment to the mess of potage we cooked in our billy-cans on the primus.

The Germans were already in bed when we returned. I went my solitary way to my lonely barracks room. The moon rose high in the darkened sky and slanted ghostly rays through my prison windows. I decided to sleep in my jeans. I dozed for a while, then shot fully awake at a noise coming from somewhere in the far corner of the building where I had originally been meant to sleep. I sat bolt upright and listened. Not a sound from the five flowers of manhood two rooms down the corridor. I sat for a long time, my face cupped on my knees. I consoled myself that I had had a bad dream and settled down, but when the eerie howling rose and fell once more I was out of the bunk, stubbing my toe as I fled down the corridor to where the five lads were sleeping. Snores greeted me as I barged in the door of the men's dorm, but their heads shot up when I unceremoniously fell over one of the German's rucksacks. On cue, the weird howling started again.

'Do you hear that?' I demanded. I couldn't see their faces clearly in the moonlit room, but I sensed their exasperation as the five of them burrowed down again. Tom's head resurfaced.

'I'm not sleeping up there on my own,' I whispered as I scuttled to the far end of the room. The noise rose again and was answered by a prolonged wailing. A sleepy voice from the corner bunk consoled me in a drawling Limerick accent, 'It's only an oul' dog sittin' on his tail, Phil. Will ye get to sleep outa that.'

The warden had locked his dog in a small room just beyond the women's section. 'He did that deliberately,' I said next morning as we were setting out to meet the bus. 'I'm sure he did it to spite us.' None of the males were prepared to concede that, but they all agreed that it was better if I stayed in their dorm, and the warden in his wisdom never queried our sleeping arrangements. Though we didn't enlighten him, somehow the whole village knew. When we boarded the bus again the following day, Madame le wife creased her face in a huge grin and wagged her finger at Tom and me.

'*La couchette*,' she cackled to the great interest of the poultry-laden, bread-basketted, flat-capped occupants of the bus. '*La couchette*,' she squealed as she rolled along beside us to the hostel door. Just as well my mother is not around, I thought; she would be having forty fits. And all this so close to the holy town of Lourdes.

We travelled into Lourdes each day on the bus, doing all the exercises necessary for a pilgrimage. We attended the blessing of the sick, climbed the Way of the Cross, spent silent time at the grotto and trailed through the hundreds of shops, but because of the time of the village bus we were unable to take part in the torchlight procession. Before we left an uncomplicated priest blessed our medals and rosaries as they lay beneath the bread and food in our bags: a man after my own heart. Once more we were on the train to

Paris, looking back at a river of lanterns winding in procession to the grotto. We lowered the window of the train and listened as a thousand voices rose in songs of praise, the sound fading into the night as we began our homeward journey.

15
New Beginnings

N OW THAT MY mother had me safely home, she insisted that I drink milk and stout every day to build me up for the months ahead. 'Stop making faces,' she said when I baulked at the bitter mixture, 'because you'll get it every day before your dinner. It's the best tonic there is.' Her words brought me back years, to the weeks after Nance my youngest sister was born, when my father said the exact same words to my mother. It made me sad. I was the first to fly the nest and my wedding would be another big break in the family.

The nights closed in quickly after our return from France. It was good to be home, I decided, as I sat one evening curled up on the sofa before the kitchen range, on my knee a list of the things still to be done for the wedding. The Sacred Heart lamp, its wick newly trimmed and its brass bowl replenished with paraffin, glowed in the semi-darkness. The slice of bread I was toasting at the bars of the grate singed and burned, and I scraped the marks of the bars onto the Home-Sweet-Home fender and listened to the autumn rain thundering on the corrugated-iron roof of the old shed my father had built.

Everything was going well for the wedding and I had reason to be content. Most things were in hand. Betty and Tess had been consulted about their bridesmaids' dresses and Jennie in her convent would ice the wedding-cake which would be baked in the traditional way by a woman who had been making them for twenty-five years and had never had a failure, or so I was told.

Tom and I were attending night-classes in the technical school to prepare us to become good homemakers. This was an accepted part of a couple's preparation for marriage, and all of us in my domestic science classes had visions of beautiful homes which we would adorn with our own skills. We slip-stitched, cross-stitched, french-knotted and drew threadwork on tray cloths, preparing for every occasion from the visit of the parish priest to special tea-parties. Tom had joined a woodwork class, where husbands-to-be were initiated in the mysteries of making kitchen tables, which usually rocked on their legs, or bedside lockers with swinging doors which never quite closed. On Saturdays they were to be found in hardware shops with long lists of materials and measurements noted on scraps of paper, and they were tenderly dealt with by assistants in brown shop-coats who could spot amateurs at a hundred paces.

But there was one important point we had failed to notice when we had selected our date. It was a Friday, a day of abstinence.

'Fish,' my mother said.

'Or eggs,' Madge suggested helpfully.

'Over my dead body,' I said. 'I'm not having a wedding breakfast of either fish or eggs and what's more, I'm not going to change the date either.' Marriages were celebrated in the mornings, usually at 9 a.m., and in reality the wedding breakfast afterwards was a four-course lunch. It was clear that we would have to seek a dispensation to allow us to eat meat.

'He'll dig in his heels again and refuse permission,' Tom said, 'like he did when you suggested that you wanted Father Condren to officiate.' We had been annoyed about that, but my old friend Father Condren had counselled forbearance and told us that he would be with us on the altar on the day. Nearly ten years previously the same curate had refused Tom permission when he had wanted to attend Trinity College. Tom had accepted the decision then as he thought he should.

'We'll get around this one,' I said to Tom. 'The reception is not being held in the parish, so surely it is the responsibility of the parish priest where the meal is being eaten.' I was right. We approached that parish priest who was the soul of kindness and consideration, nodded gravely when we told him of our difficulty, and granted us a dispensation on the spot.

'Do I really need a trousseau?' I was in my favourite spot again, toasting my toes at the kitchen range.

174

'Yes,' my mother said. 'It's your last chance to spend your own money, so spoil yourself. When you're married you will be dependent on your husband for all your needs. Most girls buy enough clothes to last them for at least two years, and sometimes even longer.' I didn't mind spoiling myself, but I objected strongly to the custom which said that my trousseau had to be displayed in full to all my friends when they gathered for my hen party.

'Nobody wants to see your trousseau,' I said to Deirdre when we looked through the list of things she would need when she entered the convent.

'It's not as exciting as yours,' she said, 'and there's going to be very little of it.' She had been instructed not to go to much expense in case she changed her mind, which was very sensible and eliminated the long list of items which most nuns and priests were asked to bring when they left home. We went over her requirements with much giggling. I made her her postulant's gown, black with a small cape, and we shopped for black shoes and stockings and a stock of underclothes.

The evening before she entered the convent, Tom called to say goodbye and take a last photograph of Deirdre in her postulant's garb, and then he left us together. I spent that night in the flat while she wrote notes and letters to the many friends she was leaving behind. As I watched her I had time to reflect on the huge step she was taking, a step which could so easily have been mine. We had one last meal together.

The following day produced the worst floods in living memory. Deirdre was due in the convent at four o'clock and though the little rivers of Dublin were overflowing we decided that one last walk through the city was what we needed. A small amount of sherry remained in the bottle Deirdre had bought the previous week to entertain her friends and we shared it between us, then readied her suitcase and set off through the rain which beat down with relentless intensity. We walked down Herbert Street past the canal and on to the Rathmines Road, our shoes squelching on the pavement. At the top of Rathmines I checked the time on the Town Hall clock.

'We've time for a bowl of soup,' I said, 'let's go to the Red Shoes.' In the café we cupped our hands around the steaming bowls and took stock. We were both wet and bedraggled, but Deirdre, with her short bobbed hair and her eyes bright in her beautiful face, was showing none of the nervousness I was dreading.

'It's a quarter to four,' she said, grasping her case. 'Let's go.'

I passed the proprietor a five-pound note and he rooted for change. 'I'll come back for it,' I said and I rushed out after Deirdre who had disappeared on to the main road. We ran the rest of the way to the convent gate. We pulled the bell outside the old farm-house door and it opened silently before us. A voice within gave us the traditional greeting, 'Praise be Jesus Christ.'

'It's Deirdre.'

'Is there somebody with you?' asked the Novice Mistress, invisible behind the parlour screen.

'It's Phil,' I said and the calm voice continued, 'Say goodbye now, Phil; you will never see Deirdre again.'

We concentrated on the door into the enclosure. Deirdre gripped the handle and pushed. She turned and looked at me and was gone. The door closed behind her and I was left alone.

The proprietor of the Red Shoes looked at me in concern. 'What's wrong?' he said as he handed over my change. I shook my head, tears streaming down my face. Would he have understood? I stumbled out the door and into the dusk of a dark December day.

A white hoar-frost covered the ground early on the eleventh of February.

'A morning to skin you alive,' my Uncle Tom described it when he arrived to escort me to the church. He looked resplendent in his morning-suit. It would have been his first time ever wearing formal clothes and his chest expanded with the importance of the occasion and the part he was to play in it.

Close neighbours called to wish us well and were invited to sip a glass of sherry while they waited for the bride to appear. My mother had what I called her 'mother of sorrows' face on as she rushed around.

'It's a wedding, Mam,' Betty said as she adjusted the earrings Tom had presented to the two bridesmaids to match their pale mauve, full-length dresses.

'Straighten your headdress,' my mother snapped back, 'the car will be here shortly.'

Betty and Tess smoothed the fine net of their dresses and picked up their bouquets of yellow and mauve crocus-heads. A bouquet for the bride was not fashionable then. I carried a marriage prayer-book covered in the white satin of my dress, which held a spray of white camelias, fern and trailing white ribbons.

The house, silent and empty when my mother and two brides-maids left, was a challenge to Uncle Tom, but he cracked every joke in his repertoire, determined that no tears would be shed when finally he opened the front door. The road was empty. We knew that Tom's car had left for the church. From their front gates neighbours called 'God bless' and 'Good luck' as we made our path to the car.

The frost had thawed, but the people gathered at the church were huddled in winter coats. Betty and Tess bravely waited in the cold porch to adjust the long veil which shadowed my face. My mother beamed happily as she surveyed the three of us, the tension of the last hours forgotten. Uncle Tom straightened his shoulders and offered me his arm. The organ played. I could see Tom taking a sneaking look down the aisle before he was poked to attention by his best man. The early morning sun inched through the stained-glass windows and created a pool of light at the altar steps. Betty and Tess lifted the fine tulle veil from my face. Uncle Tom relinquished his grip on my arm, stepped back, and Tom stepped in beside me.

When our plane touched down in London the whole of England was wrapped in a mantle of snow. We had toyed with the idea of a honeymoon in the Alps but the alpine weather had obligingly come to our doorstep, and snow-filled winds billowed and blew us along London's streets. There was much in London we wanted to see and we were glad of the comfort of our hotel in Russell Square each evening, though we were soon irked by the manoeverings of the head waiter who each day ensured that we sat at a different table in the dining-room. He was a Jeeves-like character but with none of the generous humanity of that legendary figure. He ruled the dining-room with disdain for his staff and a hauteur towards the guests whom he swept to where he wanted them to sit. His game soon became very clear as we watched him: it was designed to ensure that he presented the bills and collected all tips. On our third day we firmly indicated the table which we wanted. The morning before, we had noticed an organ-grinder outside the window, wrapped in a muffler which circled his face and wound around his cap. He cranked the handle of his ancient instrument and the wavering, tumbling notes of his repertoire trembled on the frosty air as he played the Neapolitan love-song, 'Santa Lucia', and wound out the strains of 'Come Back to Sorrento'.

Then say not goodbye, come back again beloved,
Back to Sorrento, or I must die.

To the utter confusion of the major-domo of the dining-room we insisted on our street-side table and lapped up the organ-grinder's romantic tunes, 'By the Light of the Silvery Moon', 'Pale Hands I Loved', 'The Vine-Covered Chapel on the Hill'. Every morning after breakfast we rounded the corner and placed our coins in his felt bag, but one morning he was not in his usual spot. We found him in Bedford Place.

'Moved on, Miss,' he said when we enquired. 'Some big nob in the hotel didn't like me outside the dining-room window.'

The extreme weather conditions were replicated in Dublin when our plane eventually touched down. I thought of my mother waiting anxiously in our new home in Churchtown to welcome us back; she would be aware of the dire warnings of bad weather, but would not know our plane had been delayed. No telephone lines had been laid in the new housing areas and wouldn't be for a long time.

There were lights blazing and a great coal fire roaring up the chimney to greet us when the taxi crunched over the rutted roadway as we swung in from the Braemor Road. The house was full with members of both our families and all the trimmings of a party had been prepared, but the weather ruled out all partying. The bus terminus for the city was nearly a mile away and the last bus left just after ten o'clock. Half an hour after we arrived, Tom and I reluctantly waved goodbye to our visitors and watched them trudge up the road and through the little laneway at the top of the Gardens. We turned to face the brightness, the newness and the silence of our new home.

The eerie quiet that comes with snow was broken next morning by the croaking of a frog in the ditch which ran at the end of our garden, the twittering of anxious birds searching for food and the screeching of seagulls sweeping in from the nearby coastline. These were not the sounds we were used to. Nor was the noise which came clearly through the bedroom window, the distant chug-chugging of the Bray train as it made its way past Dundrum and down to Miltown station.

Two days later the snowstorm which had started on the evening of our wedding gave way to brilliant sunshine. For Tom it was back to the office, and he joined other new husbands to cycle companionably to their various jobs in the city. Those without bicycles or not inclined to tackle the five-mile cycle headed in ones and twos for the morning bus, which could not be missed or a half-day's salary might be lost, or joined the walkers to the train-station at Dundrum.

There was little for me to do each day, except my cleaning and housekeeping in a house much larger than either of our previous homes, and spotlessly new. Fifty houses had been planned in our cul-de-sac, set around an open space with an entrance from the main road and no through road for traffic, but not all of the houses were finished and the empty space was a muddy, deeply-rutted builder's dumping-ground. The site had once been in the grounds of Landscape Manor. Without my bicycle I was isolated from family and friends. Strangely the day never seemed long as spring came and the evenings lengthened. We held lots of house-warming parties, help-in-the-garden parties, and relatives and friends were glad of an opportunity to call, though some of them thought we were crazy to want to live so far from what they called 'civilisation', although town was slowly meeting country.

The little hamlet of Churchtown lay in the heart of open land, with the Castle Golfcourse running onto the lands of Rathfarnham Castle and sheltering us on one side, while further on were the fruit fields of Lamb Brothers, the jam manufacturers. Hedged all round by sprawling fields and farmland, Tom and I revelled in the sense of country living. We were awakened each morning by the call of a corncrake who nested somewhere in the grass hummocks amongst the builder's rubble, and the intermittent crying of new-born babies coming through the open bedroom windows of our neighbours' houses.

When the back-garden finally had to be tackled, Tom listened intently to the advice doled out in a lilting Cork accent by our next-door neighbour, whose own contribution to horticulture was to lean on our wall, tilt his cap back on his head and ponder both our plots. One evening Tom found a helper for another of our neighbours. He discovered a hedgehog at our front gate and gingerly carried it to the corner house on the palm of his spade, where it was welcomed, if not with open arms, then with great enthusiasm to rid the garden of an army of slugs.

We had neither 'chapel nor meeting house' in Churchtown, but we boasted our own cinema which did fair trade with the burgeoning local population. On fine days my front door would stand wide open while I swept builder's dust into neat piles and exchanged greetings with whoever passed. Shops were scattered over a radius of half a mile and it was there, more often than not, that you would meet a neighbour and walk home together. Nobody was an island. The open doorways, the cry of a baby, the men leaning on their spades and exchanging plants over garden walls, were the signs of a village community, Catholic, Protestant and Jew, growing together, with new ideas, new thoughts and new families, in an atmosphere of trust and neighbourliness.

Summer melted into autumn and our thoughts turned to the cold winds of winter and the bleak mornings which Tom would spend cycling or trudging to catch transport to the city. When we arrived in Churchtown a lone car had stuttered down the road each morning, but now budgets were being stretched in every house so that the breadwinner might have a car, and the peace of early mornings was punctuated with the cranking of starting handles and the revving of engines.

'I've bought a car,' Tom announced casually one evening as he wheeled his bicycle past me into the garage.

'We can't afford a car,' I said laughingly.

'We can afford this one,' he said with a smug grin. 'I've struck a bargain.'

'How much?'

'£90 for the car, but only £45 to us. I've agreed to share with Padraig.'

'But Padraig can't drive.'

'No, but he'll learn pretty soon when he knows that I'm not going to spend my time collecting him.' Padraig and his wife lived two miles beyond us in Rathfarnham and we went over to tell them our plan.

'We bought Cormac's Ford 8,' we said. 'Why don't we alternate at weekends and travel to the office together during the week? It will halve the expense.'

It was a crazy idea but it worked. So did the car, for a few months anyway, and by then a new ambition had been born.